Which draw the dayes of men forth in extent;
Or th' auncient genius of that citie brent;
But seeing her so piteouslie perplexed,
I (to her calling) askt what her so vexed.

'Ah! what delight,' quoth she, 'in earthlie thing,
Or comfort can I, wretched creature, have?
Whose happines the heavens envying,
From highest staire to lowest step me drave,
And have in mine owne bowels made my grave,
That of all nations now I am forlorne,
The worlds sad spectacle, and Fortunes scorne.'

Much was I mooved at her piteous plaint,
And felt my heart nigh riven in my brest
With tender ruth to see her sore constraint;
That shedding teares a while I still did rest,
And after did her name of her request.
'Name have I none,' quoth she, 'nor anie being,
Bereft of both by Fates unjust decreeing.

'I was that citie which the garland wore
Of Britaines pride, delivered unto me
By Romane victors, which it wonne of yore;
Though nought at all but ruines now I bee,
And lye in mine owne ashes, as ye see:
Verlame I was; what bootes it that I was,
Sith now I am but weedes and wastfull gras?

'O vaine worlds glorie, and unstedfast state
Of all that lives on face of sinfull earth!
Which from their first untill their utmost date
Tast no one hower of happines or merth,
But like as at the ingate of their berth
They crying creep out of their mothers woomb,
So wailing backe go to their wofull toomb.

'Why then dooth flesh, a bubble glas of breath,
Hunt after honour and advauncement vaine,
And reare a trophee for devouring death
With so great labour and long lasting paine,
As if his daies for ever should remaine?
Sith all that in this world is great or gaie
Doth as a vapour vanish, and decaie.

'Looke backe, who list, unto the former ages,
And call to count, what is of them become:
Where be those learned wits and antique sages,
Which of all wisedome knew the perfect somme?
Where those great warriors, which did overcomme
The world with conquest of their might and maine,

And made one meare of th' earth and of their raine?

'What nowe is of th' Assyrian Lyonesse,
Of whome no footing now on earth appeares?
What of the Persian Beares outragiousnesse,
Whose memorie is quite worne out with yeares?
Who of the Grecian Libbard now ought heares,
That overran the East with greedie powre,
And left his whelps their kingdomes to devoure?

'And where is that same great seven headded beast,
That made all nations vassals of her pride,
To fall before her feete at her beheast,
And in the necke of all the world did ride?
Where doth she all that wondrous welth nowe hide?
With her own weight down pressed now shee lies,
And by her heaps her hugenesse testifies.

'O Rome, thy ruine I lament and rue,
And in thy fall my fatall overthrowe,
That whilom was, whilst heavens with equall vewe
Deignd to behold me, and their gifts bestowe,
The picture of thy pride in pompous shew:
And of the whole world as thou wast the empresse,
So I of this small Northerne world was princesse.

'To tell the beawtie of my buildings fayre,
Adornd with purest golde and precious stone,
To tell my riches, and endowments rare,
That by my foes are now all spent and gone,
To tell my forces, matchable to none,
Were but lost labour, that few would beleeve,
And with rehearsing would me more agreeve.

'High towers, faire temples, goodly theaters,
Strong walls, rich porches, princelie pallaces,
Large streetes, brave houses, sacred sepulchers,
Sure gates, sweete gardens, stately galleries
Wrought with faire pillours, and fine imageries,
All those (O pitie!) now are turnd to dust,
And overgrowen with blacke oblivions rust.

'Theretoo, for warlike power and peoples store,
In Britannie was none to match with mee,
That manie often did abie full sore:
Ne Troynovant, though elder sister shee,
With my great forces might compared bee;
That stout Pendragon to his perill felt,
Who in a siege seaven yeres about me dwelt.

'But long ere this, Bunduca Britonnesse

Complaints by Edmund Spenser

CONTAINING SUNDRIE SMALL POEMES OF THE WORLDS VANITIE WHEREOF THE NEXT PAGE
MAKETH MENTION

One of the greatest of English poets, Edmund Spenser was born in East Smithfield, London, in 1552.
He was educated in London at the Merchant Taylors' School and later at Pembroke College,
Cambridge. In 1579, he published The Shepheardes Calender, his first major work.

Edmund journeyed to Ireland in July 1580, in the service of the newly appointed Lord Deputy, Arthur
Grey, 14th Baron Grey de Wilton. His time included the terrible massacre at the Siege of Smerwick.

The epic poem, The Faerie Queene, is acknowledged as Edmund's masterpiece. The first three books
were published in 1590, and a second set of three books were published in 1596.

Indeed the reality is that Spenser, through his great talents, was able to move Poetry in a different
direction. It led to him being called a Poet's Poet and brought rich admiration from Milton, Raleigh,
Blake, Wordsworth, Keats, Byron, and Lord Tennyson, among others.

Spenser returned to Ireland and in 1591, Complaints, a collection of poems that voices complaints in
mournful or mocking tones was published.

In 1595, Spenser published Amoretti and Epithalamion. The volume contains eighty-nine sonnets.

In the following year Spenser wrote a prose pamphlet titled A View of the Present State of Ireland, a
highly inflammatory argument for the pacification and destruction of Irish culture.

On January 13th 1599 Edmund Spenser died at the age of forty-six. His coffin was carried to his
grave in Westminster Abbey by other poets, who threw many pens and pieces of poetry into his
grave followed with many tears.

Index of Contents

THE VISIONS OF BELLAY
THE VISIONS OF PETRARCH
Edmund Spenser – A Short Biography
Edmund Spenser – A Concise Bibliography

Since my late setting foorth of the Faerie Queene, finding that it hath found a favourable passage amongst you, I have sithence endevoured by all good meanes (for the better encrease and accomplishment of your delights,) to get into my handes such smale poemes of the same authors as I heard were disperst abroad in sundrie hands, and not easie to bee come by, by himselfe; some of them having bene diverslie imbeziled and purloyned from him, since his departure over sea. Of the which I have by good meanes gathered togeather these fewe pareels present, which I have caused to bee imprinted altogeather, for that they al seeme to containe like matter of argument in them, being all complaints and meditations of the worlds vanitie, verie grave and profitable. To which effect I understand that he besides wrote sundrie others, namelie, Ecclesiastes and Canticum Canticorum translated, A Senights Slumber, The Hell of Lovers, his Purgatorie, being all dedicated to ladies, so as it may seeme he ment them all to one volume: besides some other pamphlets looselie scattered abroad: as The Dying Pellican, The Howers of the Lord, The Sacrifice of a Sinner, The Seven Psalmes, &c., which when I can either by himselfe or otherwise attaine too, I meane likewise for your favour sake to set foorth. In the meane time, praying you gentlie to accept of these, and gracious-lie to entertaine the 'new poet,' I take leave.

INTRODUCTION

Though Complaints was not published till 1591, a year after the first issue of the Faery Queen, the poems of which it is composed are more properly to be classed with the Shepherd's Calendar. Most of them might have been printed, though perhaps not exactly as they now stand, before 1580; the others are best understood in company with these. The Calendar and Complaints, indeed, taken together, are the record of Spenser's growth to maturity.

The circumstances of the publication are very oddly confused. In the opening address the credit for the whole enterprise is assumed by 'the Printer,' Ponsonby, who, we are told, hunted the poems out and made up and issued the volume by his own efforts. This work, we gather, was mainly prosecuted after the poet's 'departure over sea'—his return, that is, to Ireland early in 1591. And the volume certainly was published after his 'departure.' Yet we know that it had been made ready for printing while he was still in England. It appears on the Stationers' Register for December 29, 1590, as approved by one of the official censors: at that time, therefore, the copy must have been at least approximately complete. Three of the poems, moreover, 'The Tears of the Muses,' 'Mother Hubberd's Tale,' and 'Muiopotmos,' the central poems of the volume, bear signs of having been prepared for the press by himself and issued individually—'Muiopotmos' in 1590. The plausible address of 'the Printer,' in fine, is not wholly to be trusted. What, then, is to be made of it? According to Dr. Grosart, it was devised by the poet as a blind, in the manner of Swift. For such a device one seeks a reason. May this be that, as, in 1579 (by the first letter to Harvey), he was shy of 'seeming to utter his writings for gaine and commoditie,' so now, but a year after the issue of the Faery Queen. he was loth to accept the full responsibility of a second considerable volume? Any account of the publication, however, must be very largely conjectural.

The chronology of the poems is less in doubt. Though two or three of them are somewhat hard to place, the majority can at least be grouped in certain main periods with reasonable probability. First of all is the group that belongs to his university days, 1570–1576, and his subsequent sojourn in Lancashire: 'The Visions of Petrarch,' 'The Visions of Bellay,' 'Ruins of Rome,' and, perhaps, 'Visions of the World's Vanity.' Following upon these days is what may loosely be called his first London period, during which, until it ended with his departure for Ireland in 1580, his headquarters were probably in the capital. These three years were of marked literary activity. To them belong most, if not all, of the Calendar, and presumably the greater number of his so-called 'lost works,' besides the beginnings of the Faery Queen; to them belong also some of the most important 'complaints,' 'Virgil's Gnat,' 'Mother Hubberd's Tale,' and, less certainly, 'The Tears of the Muses.' Then follow the years of service in Ireland, till Raleigh brought him back in 1589. During this period he would seem to have given his leisure for poetry almost exclusively to the Faery Queen. Of the two remaining 'complaints,' 'The Ruins of Time' was written shortly after his return to England, and 'Muiopotmos' perhaps at about the same time.

'The Ruins of Time' and 'Muiopotmos' were composed not long before publication and probably needed no retouching. 'Mother Hubberd's Tale' and 'The Tears of the Muses,' early poems, were to some extent revised for the press. The others, one may think, were allowed to appear as first finished, or were at most but casually retouched. For, from the general tenor of his output, one infers that Spenser was not very sedulous in the revision of work once completed, and these poems were relatively unimportant—all but one, translations. They are not, like their companions, dedicated to people alive and influential in 1590: their chief function, indeed, would seem to be to fill out the volume. If Ponsonby really had a share in the collecting of Complaints, it must have been these, or some of them, that he gathered.

To the reader of Complaints one name recurs more frequently than others, that of Joachim Du Bellay, who, from 1549 to his early death in 1560, was one of the leaders of the new school of poetry in France. From him Spenser translated 'The Visions of Bellay' and 'Ruins of Rome,' and from him chiefly he must have acquired those poetic theories of the Pléiade which are the staple of 'The Tears of the Muses.' Du Bellay is a personality of great attractiveness. Not so distinguished an artist as his colleague Ronsard, he had qualities of mind and character that win us more: dignity untouched by arrogance, guarded from it by native sense of fitness, the distinction of a finely congruous nature; in especial, a singularly penetrating and human melancholy. On any Elizabethan author of a volume of 'complaints' his influence might be among the deepest of that day. It is noteworthy, however, that his really central work, the Regrets, does not seem to have touched Spenser at all. And indeed, the 'life-long vein of melancholy' which Dr. Grosart detects in 'the newe poete' must have been, at best, rather thin. His elegies are hardly convincing. When he strikes the note of personal disappointment, his verse occasionally betrays a feeling akin to sadness, but the bulk of his really characteristic and genuine work is anything but sad. In the Faery Queen one may search far and wide, in vain, for a touch of that peculiar feeling which pervades the romance-epic of the genuinely melancholy Tasso. His most constant mood would seem rather to have been a serenity neither sad nor cheerful. In any case, one will not infer his temperament from the professed melancholy of his earlier work. That much of the Calendar is gloomy, that he wrote a whole volume of 'complaints,' was to have been expected: work in that vein was a convention of the days into which he was born. The cosmopolitan pastoral invited, if it did not impose, a strain of lamentation, and in England, since the days of Sir Thomas Wyatt, love-poetry in the manner and tone of the plaintive Petrarch, meditations upon the vanity of life, elegies, stories of the falls of the mighty had formed, in good measure, the staple of serious poetry. Spenser's early work but continues a convention already well established.

DEDICATED TO THE RIGHT NOBLE AND BEAUTIFULL LADIE, THE LADIE MARIE COUNTESSE OF PEMBROOKE

Most honourable and bountifull Ladie, there bee long sithens deepe sowed in my brest the seede of most entire love and humble affection unto that most brave knight, your noble brother deceased; which taking roote began in his life time some-what to bud forth, and to shew themselves to him, as then in the weakenes of their first spring: and would in their riper strength (had it pleased High God till then to drawe out his daies) spired forth fruit of more perfection. But since God hath disdeigned the world of that most noble spirit, which was the hope of all learned men, and the patron of my young Muses; togeather with him both their hope of anie further fruit was cut off, and also the tender delight of those their first blossoms nipped and quite dead. Yet sithens my late cumming into England, some frends of mine (which might much prevaile with me, and indeede commaund me) knowing with howe straight bandes of duetie I was tied to him, as also bound unto that noble house, (of which the chiefe hope then rested in him) have sought to revive them by upbraiding me, for that I have not shewed anie thankefull remembrance towards him or any of them, but suffer their names to sleep in silence and forgetfulnesse. Whome chieflie to satisfie, or els to avoide that fowle blot of unthankefulnesse, I have conceived this small poeme, intituled by a generall name of The Worlds Ruines: yet speciallie intended to the renowming of that noble race, from which both you and he sprong, and to the eternizing of some of the chiefe of them late deceased. The which I dedicate unto your Ladiship as whome it most speciallie concerneth, and to whome I acknowledge my selfe bounden, by manie singular favours and great graces. I pray for your honourable happinesse: and so humblie kisse your handes.

Your Ladiships ever humblie at commaund,

Edmund Spenser.

THE RUINES OF TIME

It chaunced me on day beside the shore
Of silver streaming Thamesis to bee,
Nigh where the goodly Verlame stood of yore,
Of which there now remaines no memorie,
Nor anie little moniment to see,
By which the travailer that fares that way
This once was she may warned be to say.

There on the other side, I did behold
A woman sitting sorrowfullie wailing,
Rending her yeolow locks, like wyrie golde
About her shoulders careleslie downe trailing,
And streames of teares from her faire eyes forth railing.
In her right hand a broken rod she held,
Which towards heaven shee seemd on high to weld.

Whether she were one of that rivers nymphes,
Which did the losse of some dere love lament,
I doubt; or one of those three fatall impes

Her mightie hoast against my bulwarkes brought,
Bunduca, that victorious conqueresse,
That, lifting up her brave heroïck thought
Bove womens weaknes, with the Romanes fought,
Fought, and in field against them thrice prevailed:
Yet was she foyld, when as she me assailed.

'And though at last by force I conquered were
Of hardie Saxons, and became their thrall,
Yet was I with much bloodshed bought full deere,
And prizde with slaughter of their generall:
The moniment of whose sad funerall,
For wonder of the world, long in me lasted;
But now to nought, through spoyle of time, is wasted.

'Wasted it is, as if it never were,
And all the rest that me so honord made,
And of the world admired ev'rie where,
Is turnd to smoake, that doth to nothing fade;
And of that brightnes now appeares no shade,
But greislie shades, such as doo haunt in hell
With fearfull fiends, that in deep darknes dwell.

'Where my high steeples whilom usde to stand,
On which the lordly faulcon wont to towre,
There now is but an heap of lyme and sand,
For the shriche-owle to build her balefull bowre:
And where the nightingale wont forth to powre
Her restles plaints, to comfort wakefull lovers,
There now haunt yelling mewes and whining plovers.

'And where the christall Thamis wont to slide
In silver channell, downe along the lee,
About whose flowrie bankes on either side
A thousand nymphes, with mirthfull jollitee,
Were wont to play, from all annoyance free,
There now no rivers course is to be seene,
But moorish fennes, and marshes ever greene.

'Seemes that that gentle river, for great griefe
Of my mishaps, which oft I to him plained,
Or for to shunne the horrible mischiefe,
With which he saw my cruell foes me pained,
And his pure streames with guiltles blood oft stained,
From my unhappie neighborhood farre fled,
And his sweete waters away with him led.

'There also where the winged ships were seene
In liquid waves to cut their fomie waie,
And thousand fishers numbred to have been,
In that wide lake looking for plenteous praie

Of fish, which they with baits usde to betraie,
Is now no lake, nor anie fishers store,
Nor ever ship shall saile there anie more.

'They all are gone, and all with them is gone:
Ne ought to me remaines, but to lament
My long decay, which no man els doth mone,
And mourne my fall with dolefull dreriment.
Yet it is comfort in great languishment,
To be bemoned with compassion kinde,
And mitigates the anguish of the minde.

'But me no man bewaileth, but in game,
Ne sheddeth teares from lamentable eie:
Nor anie lives that mentioneth my name
To be remembred of posteritie,
Save one, that maugre Fortunes injurie,
And Times decay, and Envies cruell tort,
Hath writ my record in true-seeming sort.

'Cambden, the nourice of antiquitie,
And lanterne unto late succeeding age,
To see the light of simple veritie
Buried in ruines, through the great outrage
Of her owne people, led with warlike rage,
Cambden, though Time all moniments obscure,
Yet thy just labours ever shall endure.

'But whie (unhappie wight) doo I thus crie,
And grieve that my remembrance quite is raced
Out of the knowledge of posteritie,
And all my antique moniments defaced?
Sith I doo dailie see things highest placed,
So soone as Fates their vitall thred have shorne,
Forgotten quite as they were never borne.

'It is not long, since these two eyes beheld
A mightie Prince, of most renowmed race,
Whom England high in count of honour held,
And greatest ones did sue to gaine his grace;
Of greatest ones he greatest in his place,
Sate in the bosome of his Soveraine,
And Right and loyall did his word maintaine.

'I saw him die, I saw him die, as one
Of the meane people, and brought foorth on beare;
I saw him die, and no man left to mone
His dolefull fate that late him loved deare:
Scarse anie left to close his eylids neare;
Scarse anie left upon his lips to laie
The sacred sod, or requiem to saie.

'O trustlesse state of miserable men,
That builde your blis on hope of earthly thing,
And vainly thinke your selves halfe happie then,
When painted faces with smooth flattering
Doo fawne on you, and your wide praises sing,
And when the courting masker louteth lowe,
Him true in heart and trustie to you trow!

'All is but fained, and with oaker dide,
That everie shower will wash and wipe away,
All things doo change that under heaven abide,
And after death all friendship doth decaie.
Therefore, what ever man bearst worldlie sway,
Living, on God and on thy selfe relie;
For when thou diest, all shall with thee die.

'He now is dead, and all is with him dead,
Save what in heavens storehouse he uplaid:
His hope is faild, and come to passe his dread,
And evill men (now dead) his deeds upbraid:
Spite bites the dead, that living never baid.
He now is gone, the whiles the foxe is crept
Into the hole the which the badger swept.

'He now is dead, and all his glorie gone,
And all his greatnes vapoured to nought,
That as a glasse upon the water shone,
Which vanisht quite, so soone as it was sought:
His name is worne alreadie out of thought,
Ne anie poet seekes him to revive;
Yet manie poets honourd him alive.

'Ne doth his Colin, carelesse Colin Cloute,
Care now his idle bagpipe up to raise,
Ne tell his sorrow to the listning rout
Of shepherd groomes, which wont his songs to praise:
Praise who so list, yet I will him dispraise,
Untill he quite him of this guiltie blame:
Wake, shepheards boy, at length awake for shame!

'And who so els did goodnes by him gaine,
And who so els his bounteous minde did trie,
Whether he shepheard be, or shepheards swaine,
(For manie did, which doo it now denie)
Awake, and to his song a part applie:
And I, the whilest you mourne for his decease,
Will with my mourning plaints your plaint increase.

'He dyde, and after him his brother dyde,
His brother prince, his brother noble peere,

That whilste he lived was of none envyde,
And dead is now, as living, counted deare,
Deare unto all that true affection beare,
But unto thee most deare, O dearest dame,
His noble spouse and paragon of fame.

'He, whilest he lived, happie was through thee,
And, being dead, is happie now much more;
Living, that lincked chaunst with thee to bee,
And dead, because him dead thou dost adore
As living, and thy lost deare love deplore.
So whilst that thou, faire flower of chastitie,
Dost live, by thee thy lord shall never die.

'Thy lord shall never die, the whiles this verse
Shall live, and surely it shall live for ever:
For ever it shall live, and shall rehearse
His worthie praise, and vertues dying never,
Though death his soule doo from his bodie sever.
And thou thy selfe herein shalt also live;
Such grace the heavens doo to my verses give.

'Ne shall his sister, ne thy father die,
Thy father, that good earle of rare renowne,
And noble patrone of weake povertie;
Whose great good deeds, in countrey and in towne,
Have purchast him in heaven an happie crowne;
Where he now liveth in eternall blis,
And left his sonne t' ensue those steps of his.

'He, noble bud, his grandsires livelie hayre,
Under the shadow of thy countenaunce
Now ginnes to shoote up fast, and flourish fayre
In learned artes and goodlie governaunce,
That him to highest honour shall advaunce.
Brave impe of Bedford, grow apace in bountie,
And count of wisedome more than of thy countie.

'Ne may I let thy husbands sister die,
That goodly ladie, sith she eke did spring
Out of this stocke and famous familie,
Whose praises I to future age doo sing,
And foorth out of her happie womb did bring
The sacred brood of learning and all honour,
In whom the heavens powrde all their gifts upon her.

'Most gentle spirite breathed from above,
Out of the bosome of the Makers blis,
In whom all bountie and all vertuous love
Appeared in their native propertis,
And did enrich that noble breast of his

With treasure passing all this worldes worth,
Worthie of heaven it selfe, which brought it forth.

'His blessed spirite, full of power divine
And influence of all celestiall grace,
Loathing this sinfull earth and earthlie slime,
Fled backe too soone unto his native place,
Too soone for all that did his love embrace,
Too soone for all this wretched world, whom he
Robd of all right and true nobilitie.

'Yet ere his happie soule to heaven went
Out of this fleshlie goale, he did devise
Unto his heavenlie Maker to present
His bodie, as a spotles sacrifise;
And chose, that guiltie hands of enemies
Should powre forth th' offring of his guiltles blood:
So life exchanging for his countries good.

'O noble spirite, live there ever blessed,
The worlds late wonder, and the heavens new joy,
Live ever there, and leave me here distressed
With mortall cares, and cumbrous worlds anoy.
But where thou dost that happines enjoy,
Bid me, O bid me quicklie come to thee,
That happie there I maie thee alwaies see.

'Yet, whilest the Fates affoord me vitall breath,
I will it spend in speaking of thy praise,
And sing to thee, untill that timelie death
By heavens doome doo ende my earthlie daies:
Thereto doo thou my humble spirite raise,
And into me that sacred breath inspire,
Which thou there breathest perfect and entire.

'Then will I sing; but who can better sing
Than thine owne sister, peerles ladie bright,
Which to thee sings with deep harts sorrowing,
Sorrowing tempered with deare delight,
That her to heare I feele my feeble spright
Robbed of sense, and ravished with joy:
O sad joy, made of mourning and anoy!

'Yet will I sing; but who can better sing,
Than thou thy selfe, thine owne selfes valiance,
That, whilest thou livedst, madest the forrests ring,
And fields resownd, and flockes to leap and daunce,
And shepheards leave their lambs unto mischaunce,
To runne thy shrill Arcadian pipe to heare:
O happie were those dayes, thrice happie were!

'But now more happie thou, and wretched wee,
Which want the wonted sweetnes of thy voice,
Whiles thou now in Elisian fields so free,
With Orpheus, and with Linus, and the choice
Of all that ever did in rimes rejoyce,
Conversest, and doost heare their heavenlie layes,
And they heare thine, and thine doo better praise.

'So there thou livest, singing evermore,
And here thou livest, being ever song
Of us, which living loved thee afore,
And now thee worship, mongst that blessed throng
Of heavenlie poets and heroes strong.
So thou both here and there immortall art,
And everie where through excellent desart.

'But such as neither of themselves can sing,
Nor yet are sung of others for reward,
Die in obscure oblivion, as the thing
Which never was, ne ever with regard
Their names shall of the later age be heard,
But shall in rustie darknes ever lie,
Unles they mentiond be with infamie.

'What booteth it to have been rich alive?
What to be great? what to be gracious?
When after death no token doth survive
Of former being in this mortall hous,
But sleepes in dust dead and inglorious,
Like beast, whose breath but in his nostrels is,
And hath no hope of happinesse or blis.

'How manie great ones may remembred be,
Which in their daies most famouslie did florish,
Of whome no word we heare, nor signe now see,
But as things wipt out with a sponge to-perishe,
Because they, living, cared not to cherishe
No gentle wits, through pride or covetize,
Which might their names for ever memorize!

'Provide therefore (ye princes) whilst ye live,
That of the Muses ye may friended bee,
Which unto men eternitie do give;
For they be daughters of Dame Memorie
And Jove, the father of Eternitie,
And do those men in golden thrones repose,
Whose merits they to glorifie do chose.

'The seven fold yron gates of grislie Hell,
And horrid house of sad Proserpina,
They able are with power of mightie spell

To breake, and thence the soules to bring awaie
Out of dread darkenesse to eternall day,
And them immortall make, which els would die
In foule forgetfulnesse, and nameles lie.

'So whilome raised they the puissant brood
Of golden girt Alcmena, for great merite,
Out of the dust to which the Oetæan wood
Had him consum'd, and spent his vitall spirite,
To highest heaven, where now he doth inherite
All happinesse in Hebes silver bowre,
Chosen to be her dearest paramoure.

'So raisde they eke faire Ledaes warlick twinnes,
And interchanged life unto them lent,
That, when th' one dies, th' other then beginnes
To shew in heaven his brightnes orient;
And they, for pittie of the sad wayment,
Which Orpheus for Eurydice did make,
Her back againe to life sent for his sake.

'So happie are they, and so fortunate,
Whom the Pierian sacred sisters love,
That freed from bands of impacable fate,
And power of death, they live for aye above,
Where mortall wreakes their blis may not remove:
But with the gods, for former vertues meede,
On nectar and ambrosia do feede.

'For deeds doe die, how ever noblie donne,
And thoughts of men do as themselves decay,
But wise wordes taught in numbers for to runne,
Recorded by the Muses, live for ay,
Ne may with storming showers be washt away;
Ne bitter breathing windes with harmfull blast,
Nor age, nor envie, shall them ever wast.

'In vaine doo earthly princes then, in vaine,
Seeke with pyramides, to heaven aspired,
Or huge colosses, built with costlie paine,
Or brasen pillours, never to be fired,
Or shrines, made of the mettall most desired,
To make their memories for ever live:
For how can mortall immortalitie give?

'Such one Mausolus made, the worlds great wonder,
But now no remnant doth thereof remaine:
Such one Marcellus, but was torne with thunder:
Such one Lisippus, but is worne with raine:
Such one King Edmond, but was rent for gaine.
All such vaine moniments of earthlie masse,

Devour'd of Time, in time to nought doo passe.

'But Fame with golden wings aloft doth flie,
Above the reach of ruinous decay,
And with brave plumes doth beate the azure skie,
Admir'd of base-borne men from farre away:
Then who so will with vertuous deeds assay
To mount to heaven, on Pegasus must ride,
And with sweete poets verse be glorifide.

'For not to have been dipt in Lethe lake
Could save the sonne of Thetis from to die;
But that blinde bard did him immortall make
With verses, dipt in deaw of Castalie:
Which made the Easterne conquerour to crie,
O fortunate yong-man, whose vertue found
So brave a trompe thy noble acts to sound.

'Therefore in this halfe happie I doo read
Good Melibæ, that hath a poet got
To sing his living praises being dead,
Deserving never here to be forgot,
In spight of envie, that his deeds would spot:
Since whose decease, learning lies unregarded,
And men of armes doo wander unrewarded.

'Those two be those two great calamities,
That long agoe did grieve the noble spright
Of Salomon with great indignities;
Who whilome was alive the wisest wight:
But now his wisedome is disprooved quite:
For he that now welds all things at his will
Scorns th' one and th' other in his deeper skill.

'O griefe of griefes! O gall of all good heartes!
To see that vertue should dispised bee
Of him that first was raisde for vertuous parts,
And now, broad spreading like an aged tree,
Lets none shoot up, that nigh him planted bee.
O let the man of whom the Muse is scorned,
Nor alive nor dead, be of the Muse adorned!

'O vile worlds trust, that with such vaine illusion
Hath so wise men bewitcht and overkest,
That they see not the way of their confusion!
O vainesse to be added to the rest,
That do my soule with inward griefe infest!
Let them behold the piteous fall of mee,
And in my case their owne ensample see.

'And who so els that sits in highest seate

Of this worlds glorie, worshipped of all,
Ne feareth change of time, nor fortunes threate,
Let him behold the horror of my fall,
And his owne end unto remembrance call;
That of like ruine he may warned bee,
And in himselfe be moov'd to pittie mee.'

Thus having ended all her piteous plaint,
With dolefull shrikes shee vanished away,
That I, through inward sorrowe wexen faint,
And all astonished with deepe dismay
For her departure, had no word to say;
But sate long time in sencelesse sad affright,
Looking still, if I might of her have sight.

Which when I missed, having looked long,
My thought returned greeved home againe,
Renewing her complaint with passion strong,
For ruth of that same womans piteous paine;
Whose wordes recording in my troubled braine,
I felt such anguish wound my feeble heart,
That frosen horror ran through everie part.

So inlie greeving in my groning brest,
And deepelie muzing at her doubtfull speach,
Whose meaning much I labored foorth to wreste,
Being above my slender reasons reach,
At length, by demonstration me to teach,
Before mine eies strange sights presented were,
Like tragicke pageants seeming to appeare.

I

I saw an image, all of massie gold,
Placed on high upon an altare faire,
That all which did the same from farre beholde
Might worship it, and fall on lowest staire.
Not that great idoll might with this compaire,
To which th' Assyrian tyrant would have made
The holie brethren falslie to have praid.

But th' altare on the which this image staid
Was (O great pitie!) built of brickle clay,
That shortly the foundation decaid,
With showres of heaven and tempests worne away:
Then downe it fell, and low in ashes lay,
Scorned of everie one which by it went;
That I, it seing, dearelie did lament.

II

Next unto this a statelie towre appeared,
Built all of richest stone that might bee found,

And nigh unto the heavens in height upreared,
But placed on a plot of sandie ground:
Not that great towre which is so much renownd
For tongues confusion in Holie Writ,
King Ninus worke, might be compar'd to it.

But O vaine labours of terrestriall wit,
That buildes so stronglie on so frayle a soyle,
As with each storme does fall away and flit,
And gives the fruit of all your travailes toyle,
To be the pray of Tyme, and Fortunes spoyle!
I saw this towre fall sodainlie to dust,
That nigh with griefe thereof my heart was brust.

III
Then did I see a pleasant paradize,
Full of sweete flowres and daintiest delights,
Such as on earth man could not more devize,
With pleasures choyce to feed his cheerefull sprights:
Not that which Merlin by his magicke slights
Made for the gentle Squire, to entertaine
His fayre Belphœbe, could this gardine staine.

But O short pleasure bought with lasting paine!
Why will hereafter anie flesh delight
In earthlie blis, and joy in pleasures vaine,
Since that I sawe this gardine wasted quite,
That where it was scarce seemed anie sight?
That I, which once that beautie did beholde,
Could not from teares my melting eyes withholde.

IV
Soone after this a giaunt came in place,
Of wondrous power, and of exceeding stature,
That none durst vewe the horror of his face;
Yet was he milde of speach, and meeke of nature.
Not he, which in despight of his Creatour
With railing tearmes defied the Jewish hoast,
Might with this mightie one in hugenes boast.

For from the one he could to th' other coast
Stretch his strong thighes, and th' ocæan overstride,
And reatch his hand into his enemies hoast.
But see the end of pompe and fleshlie pride:
One of his feete unwares from him did slide,
That downe hee fell into the deepe abisse,
Where drownd with him is all his earthlie blisse.

V
Then did I see a bridge, made all of golde,
Over the sea from one to other side,

Withouten prop or pillour it t' upholde,
But like the coulored rainbowe arched wide:
Not that great arche which Trajan edifide,
To be a wonder to all age ensuing,
Was matchable to this in equall vewing.

But ah! what bootes it to see earthlie thing
In glorie or in greatnes to excell,
Sith time doth greatest things to ruine bring?
This goodlie bridge, one foote not fastned well,
Gan faile, and all the rest downe shortlie fell,
Ne of so brave a building ought remained,
That griefe thereof my spirite greatly pained.

VI
I saw two beares, as white as anie milke,
Lying together in a mightie cave,
Of milde aspect, and haire as soft as silke,
That salvage nature seemed not to have,
Nor after greedie spoyle of blood to crave:
Two fairer beasts might not elswhere be found,
Although the compast world were sought around.

But what can long abide above this ground
In state of blis, or stedfast happinesse?
The cave in which these beares lay sleeping sound
Was but earth, and with her owne weightinesse
Upon them fell, and did unwares oppresse;
That, for great sorrow of their sudden fate,
Henceforth all worlds felicitie I hate.

Much was I troubled in my heavie spright,
At sight of these sad spectacles forepast,
That all my senses were bereaved quight,
And I in minde remained sore agast,
Distraught twixt feare and pitie; when at last
I heard a voyce, which loudly to me called,
That with the suddein shrill I was appalled.

'Behold,' said it, 'and by ensample see,
That all is vanitie and griefe of minde,
Ne other comfort in this world can be,
But hope of heaven, and heart to God inclinde;
For all the rest must needs be left behinde.'
With that it bad me to the other side
To cast mine eye, where other sights I spide.

I
Upon that famous rivers further shore,
There stood a snowie swan, of heavenly hiew
And gentle kinde, as ever fowle afore;

A fairer one in all the goodlie criew
Of white Strimonian brood might no man view:
There he most sweetly sung the prophecie
Of his owne death in dolefull elegie.

At last, when all his mourning melodie
He ended had, that both the shores resounded,
Feeling the fit that him forewarnd to die,
With loftie flight above the earth he bounded,
And out of sight to highest heaven mounted,
Where now he is become an heavenly signe:
There now the joy is his, here sorrow mine.

II
Whilest thus I looked, loe! adowne the lee
I sawe an harpe, stroong all with silver twyne,
And made of golde and costlie yvorie,
Swimming, that whilome seemed to have been
The harpe on which Dan Orpheus was seene
Wylde beasts and forrests after him to lead,
But was th' harpe of Philisides now dead.

At length out of the river it was reard,
And borne above the cloudes to be divin'd,
Whilst all the way most heavenly noyse was heard
Of the strings, stirred with the warbling wind,
That wrought both joy and sorrow in my mind:
So now in heaven a signe it doth appeare,
The Harpe well knowne beside the Northern Beare.

III
Soone after this I saw on th' other side
A curious coffer made of heben wood,
That in it did most precious treasure hide,
Exceeding all this baser worldes good:
Yet through the overflowing of the flood
It almost drowned was and done to nought,
That sight thereof much griev'd my pensive thought.

At length, when most in perill it was brought,
Two angels, downe descending with swift flight,
Out of the swelling streame it lightly caught,
And twixt their blessed armes it carried quight
Above the reach of anie living sight:
So now it is transform'd into that starre,
In which all heavenly treasures locked are.

IV
Looking aside I saw a stately bed,
Adorned all with costly cloth of gold,
That might for anie princes couche be red,

And deckt with daintie flowres, as if it shold
Be for some bride, her joyous night to hold:
Therein a goodly virgine sleeping lay;
A fairer wight saw never summers day.

I heard a voyce that called farre away,
And her awaking bad her quickly dight,
For lo! her bridegrome was in readie ray
To come to her, and seeke her loves delight:
With that she started up with cherefull sight;
When suddeinly both bed and all was gone,
And I in languour left there all alone.

V
Still as I gazed, I beheld where stood
A knight all arm'd, upon a winged steed,
The same that was bred of Medusaes blood,
On which Dan Perseus, borne of heavenly seed,
The faire Andromeda from perill freed:
Full mortally this knight ywounded was,
That streames of blood foorth flowed on the gras.

Yet was he deckt (small joy to him, alas!)
With manie garlands for his victories,
And with rich spoyles, which late he did purchas
Through brave atcheivements from his enemies:
Fainting at last through long infirmities,
He smote his steed, that straight to heaven him bore,
And left me here his losse for to deplore.

VI
Lastly, I saw an arke of purest golde
Upon a brazen pillour standing hie,
Which th' ashes seem'd of some great prince to hold,
Enclosde therein for endles memorie
Of him whom all the world did glorifie:
Seemed the heavens with the earth did disagree,
Whether should of those ashes keeper bee.

At last me seem'd wing footed Mercurie,
From heaven descending to appease their strife,
The arke did beare with him above the skie,
And to those ashes gave a second life,
To live in heaven, where happines is rife:
At which the earth did grieve exceedingly,
And I for dole was almost like to die.

L'ENVOY
Immortall spirite of Philisides,
Which now art made the heavens ornament,
That whilome wast the worldes chiefst riches,

Give leave to him that lov'de thee to lament
His losse, by lacke of thee to heaven hent,
And with last duties of this broken verse,
Broken with sighes, to decke thy sable herse.

And ye, faire ladie, th' honor of your daies
And glorie of the world, your high thoughts scorne,
Vouchsafe this moniment of his last praise
With some few silver dropping teares t' adorne:
And as ye be of heavenlie off-spring borne,
So unto heaven let your high minde aspire,
And loath this drosse of sinfull worlds desire.

FINIS.

THE TEARES OF THE MUSES - TO THE RIGHT HONORABLE THE LADIE STRANGE

Most brave and noble Ladie, the things that make ye so much honored of the world as ye bee, are such as (without my simple lines testimonie) are throughlie knowen to all men; namely, your excellent beautie, your vertuous behavior, and your noble match with that most honourable lord, the verie paterne of right nobilitie: but the causes for which ye have thus deserved of me to be honoured (if honour it be at all) are, both your particular bounties, and also some private bands of affinitie, which it hath pleased your Ladiship to acknowledge. Of which whenas I found my selfe in no part worthie, I devised this last slender meanes, both to intimate my humble affection to your Ladiship, and also to make the same universallie knowen to the world; that by honouring you they might know me, and by knowing me they might honor you. Vouchsafe, noble Lady, to accept this simple remembrance, thogh not worthy of your self, yet such as perhaps, by good acceptance therof, ye may hereafter cull out a more meet and memorable evidence of your own excellent deserts. So recommending the same to your Ladiships good liking, I humbly take leave.
Your Ladiships humbly ever

Edmund Spenser.

To what period this poem may belong has been somewhat disputed. On the whole, it would seem, like 'Mother Hubberd's Tale,' to be early work revised, for though the allusions in the lament of Thalia refer that passage to 1589 or 1590, there are good grounds for believing that the poem first took form before 1580. Its doleful account of the state of literature, for instance, is quite at odds with that survey in Colin Clout's Come Home Again (of 1591) wherein Spenser deals so sympathetically with his fellow poets, and is not unlike in tone to various passages in the Calendar. One can hardly understand, moreover, how, in 1590, even as a matter of convention, he could take so dismal a view of English literature. In 1580, on the other hand, before Sidney, Greene, Marlowe, and their fellows of the first great generation had begun to write, when, Spenser himself excepted, Lyly with his Euphues was the one brilliant name in English letters, such a view is quite conceivable. The matter might be argued much further, to the same result. The general tone of the poem, its mental attitude, cannot but impress a modern reader somewhat unpleasantly. The complaint that 'mightie peeres' no longer care for the immortality which only poets can confer, that poets and scholars, 'the learned,' are left without patronage, may be set down partly to a trying personal experience. The note of contempt, however, and of arrogance that one is glad to believe youthful, the complaint of universal vulgarity, the cry that Ignorance and Barbarism have quite laid waste the fair realm of the Muses—all this comes near, in the end, to seeming insufferable. If the Areopagus, the select literary club in which Sidney and Dyer and Fulke Greville, with perhaps Spenser himself, discussed the condition of English letters and planned great reforms, if this cénacle is fairly represented by 'The Tears of the Muses,' it must have been, one thinks, a more than usually supercilious clique of young radicals. Yet what may be distasteful in the poem is not so much the underlying opinions, which for 1579 or 1580 are quite intelligible, as the particular tone or mood. In this one almost suspects an echo of Ronsard. For in the great movement by which, thirty years before the Areopagus and in much the same way, the Pléiade endeavored to regenerate French literature, Ronsard is notably distinguished from his colleagues by an odd faculty for making their common views offensive or ridiculous. His rampant egotism and utter deficiency in the sense of humor lured him at times, like his greater descendant Victor Hugo, into strange extravagances. Now, the members of the Areopagus knew the poets of the Pléiade well, especially Ronsard and Du Bellay. They seem to have felt that their own problem in England was not unlike that which these men had met in France. In them they found ideals with which they sympathized, opinions which seemed to be of value for their own difficulties. That the poet was directly inspired of God (or the gods), that great men could obtain immortality from the poets alone, that poetry must go hand in hand with learning, that the arch enemy of the Muses was Ignorance, that poetry in their day languished because the great were given over to luxury and the vulgar would listen only to a horde of unlearned and base rhymesters,—these theories of the Pléiade and various precepts for the elevation of their own mother tongue to a place beside the tongues of Greece and Rome were caught at by the youthful members of the Areopagus with very lively interest. In the work of Spenser they may be traced unmistakably, chiefly in 'October,' 'The Ruins of Time,' and 'The Tears of the Muses.' This last, unhappily, voices them in a tone which, as so often in Ronsard and rarely in Du Bellay, makes sympathy quite impossible.]

THE TEARES OF THE MUSES

Rehearse to me, ye sacred sisters nine,
The golden brood of great Apolloes wit,
Those piteous plaints and sorowfull sad tine,
Which late ye powred forth as ye did sit
Beside the silver springs of Helicone,
Making your musick of hart-breaking mone.

For since the time that Phœbus foolish sonne,
Ythundered through Joves avengefull wrath,
For traversing the charret of the Sunne
Beyond the compasse of his pointed path,
Of you, his mournfull sisters, was lamented,
Such mournfull tunes were never since invented.

Nor since that faire Calliope did lose
Her loved twinnes, the dearlings of her joy,
Her Palici, whom her unkindly foes,
The Fatall Sisters, did for spight destroy,
Whom all the Muses did bewaile long space,
Was ever heard such wayling in this place.

For all their groves, which with the heavenly noyses
Of their sweete instruments were wont to sound,
And th' hollow hills, from which their silver voyces
Were wont redoubled echoes to rebound,
Did now rebound with nought but rufull cries,
And yelling shrieks throwne up into the skies.

The trembling streames which wont in chanels cleare
To romble gently downe with murmur soft,
And were by them right tunefull taught to beare
A bases part amongst their consorts oft,
Now forst to overflowe with brackish teares,
With troublous noyse did dull their daintie eares.

The joyous nymphes and lightfoote faeries
Which thether came to heare their musick sweet,
And to the measure of their melodies
Did learne to move their nimble shifting feete,
Now hearing them so heavily lament,
Like heavily lamenting from them went.

And all that els was wont to worke delight
Through the divine infusion of their skill,
And all that els seemd faire and fresh in sight,
So made by nature for to serve their will,
Was turned now to dismall heavinesse,
Was turned now to dreadfull uglinesse.

Ay me! what thing on earth, that all thing breeds,
Might be the cause of so impatient plight?
What furie, or what feend with felon deeds
Hath stirred up so mischievous despight?
Can griefe then enter into heavenly harts,
And pierce immortall breasts with mortall smarts?

Vouchsafe ye then, whom onely it concernes,
To me those secret causes to display;
For none but you, or who of you it learnes,
Can rightfully aread so dolefull lay.
Begin, thou eldest sister of the crew,
And let the rest in order thee ensew.

CLIO.
Heare, thou great Father of the Gods on hie,
That most art dreaded for thy thunder darts:
And thou our syre, that raignst in Castalie
And Mount Parnasse, the god of goodly arts:
Heare and behold the miserable state
Of us thy daughters, dolefull desolate.

Behold the fowle reproach and open shame,

The which is day by day unto us wrought
By such as hate the honour of our name,
The foes of learning and each gentle thought;
They, not contented us themselves to scorne,
Doo seeke to make us of the world forlorne.

Ne onely they that dwell in lowly dust,
The sonnes of darknes and of ignoraunce;
But they whom thou, great Jove, by doome unjust
Didst to the type of honour earst advaunce;
They now, puft up with sdeignfull insolence,
Despise the brood of blessed Sapience.

The sectaries of my celestiall skill,
That wont to be the worlds chiefe ornament,
And learned impes that wont to shoote up still,
And grow to hight of kingdomes government,
They underkeep, and with their spredding armes
Doo beat their buds, that perish through their harmes.

It most behoves the honorable race
Of mightie peeres true wisedome to sustaine,
And with their noble countenaunce to grace
The learned forheads, without gifts or gaine:
Or rather learnd themselves behoves to bee;
That is the girlond of nobilitie.

But ah! all otherwise they doo esteeme
Of th' heavenly gift of wisdomes influence,
And to be learned it a base thing deeme;
Base minded they that want intelligence:
For God himselfe for wisedome most is praised,
And men to God thereby are nighest raised.

But they doo onely strive themselves to raise
Through pompous pride, and foolish vanitie;
In th' eyes of people they put all their praise,
And onely boast of armes and auncestrie:
But vertuous deeds, which did those armes first give
To their grandsyres, they care not to atchive.

So I, that doo all noble feates professe
To register, and sound in trump of gold,
Through their bad dooings, or base slothfulnesse,
Finde nothing worthie to be writ, or told:
For better farre it were to hide their names,
Than telling them to blazon out their blames.

So shall succeeding ages have no light
Of things forepast, nor moniments of time,
And all that in this world is worthie hight

Shall die in darknesse, and lie hid in slime:
Therefore I mourne with deep harts sorrowing,
Because I nothing noble have to sing.

With that she raynd such store of streaming teares,
That could have made a stonie heart to weep,
And all her sisters rent their golden heares,
And their faire faces with salt humour steep.
So ended shee: and then the next anew
Began her grievous plaint, as doth ensew.

MELPOMENE.
O who shall powre into my swollen eyes
A sea of teares that never may be dryde,
A brasen voice that may with shrilling cryes
Pierce the dull heavens and fill the ayer wide,
And yron sides that sighing may endure,
To waile the wretchednes of world impure?

Ah, wretched world! the den of wickednesse,
Deformd with filth and fowle iniquitie;
Ah, wretched world! the house of heavinesse,
Fild with the wreaks of mortall miserie;
Ah, wretched world, and all that is therein!
The vassals of Gods wrath, and slaves of sin.

Most miserable creature under sky
Man without understanding doth appeare;
For all this worlds affliction he thereby,
And Fortunes freakes, is wisely taught to beare:
Of wretched life the onely joy shee is,
And th' only comfort in calamities.

She armes the brest with constant patience
Against the bitter throwes of dolours darts,
She solaceth with rules of sapience
The gentle minds, in midst of worldlie smarts:
When he is sad, shee seeks to make him merie,
And doth refresh his sprights when they be werie.

But he that is of reasons skill bereft,
And wants the staffe of wisedome him to stay,
Is like a ship in midst of tempest left
Withouten helme or pilot her to sway:
Full sad and dreadfull is that ships event:
So is the man that wants intendiment.

Whie then doo foolish men so much despize
The precious store of this celestiall riches?
Why doo they banish us, that patronize
The name of learning? Most unhappie wretches!

The which lie drowned in deep wretchednes,
Yet doo not see their owne unhappines.

My part it is and my professed skill
The stage with tragick buskin to adorne,
And fill the scene with plaint and outcries shrill
Of wretched persons, to misfortune borne:
But none more tragick matter I can finde
Than this, of men depriv'd of sense and minde.

For all mans life me seemes a tragedy,
Full of sad sights and sore catastrophees;
First comming to the world with weeping eye,
Where all his dayes, like dolorous trophees,
Are heapt with spoyles of fortune and of feare,
And he at last laid forth on balefull beare.

So all with rufull spectacles is fild,
Fit for Megera or Persephone;
But I, that in true tragedies am skild,
The flowre of wit, finde nought to busie me:
Therefore I mourne, and pitifully mone,
Because that mourning matter I have none.

Then gan she wofully to waile, and wring
Her wretched hands in lamentable wise;
And all her sisters, thereto answering,
Threw forth lowd shrieks and drerie dolefull cries.
So rested she: and then the next in rew
Began her grievous plaint, as doth ensew.

THALIA.
Where be the sweete delights of learnings treasure,
That wont with comick sock to beautefie
The painted theaters, and fill with pleasure
The listners eyes, and eares with melodie;
In which I late was wont to raine as queene,
And maske in mirth with graces well beseene?

O, all is gone! and all that goodly glee,
Which wont to be the glorie of gay wits,
Is layd abed, and no where now to see;
And in her roome unseemly Sorrow sits,
With hollow browes and greisly countenaunce,
Marring my joyous gentle dalliaunce.

And him beside sits ugly Barbarisme,
And brutish Ignorance, ycrept of late
Out of dredd darknes of the deep abysme,
Where being bredd, he light and heaven does hate:
They in the mindes of men now tyrannize,

And the faire scene with rudenes foule disguize.

All places they with follie have possest,
And with vaine toyes the vulgare entertaine;
But me have banished, with all the rest
That whilome wont to wait upon my traine,
Fine Counterfesaunce and unhurtfull Sport,
Delight and Laughter deckt in seemly sort.

All these, and all that els the comick stage
With seasoned wit and goodly pleasance graced,
By which mans life in his likest image
Was limned forth, are wholly now defaced;
And those sweete wits which wont the like to frame
Are now despizd, and made a laughing game.

And he, the man whom Nature selfe had made
To mock her selfe, and truth to imitate,
With kindly counter under mimick shade,
Our pleasant Willy, ah! is dead of late:
With whom all joy and jolly meriment
Is also deaded, and in dolour drent.

In stead thereof scoffing Scurrilitie,
And scornfull Follie with Contempt is crept,
Rolling in rymes of shameles ribaudrie
Without regard, or due decorum kept;
Each idle wit at will presumes to make,
And doth the learneds taske upon him take.

But that same gentle spirit, from whose pen
Large streames of honnie and sweete nectar flowe,
Scorning the boldnes of such base-borne men,
Which dare their follies forth so rashlie throwe,
Doth rather choose to sit in idle cell,
Than so himselfe to mockerie to sell.

So am I made the servant of the manie,
And laughing stocke of all that list to scorne,
Not honored nor cared for of anie;
But loath'd of losels as a thing forlorne:
Therefore I mourne and sorrow with the rest,
Untill my cause of sorrow be redrest.

Therewith she lowdly did lament and shrike,
Pouring forth streames of teares abundantly;
And all her sisters, with compassion like,
The breaches of her singulfs did supply.
So rested shee: and then the next in rew
Began her grievous plaint, as doth ensew.

EUTERPE.
Like as the dearling of the summers pryde,
Faire Philomele, when winters stormie wrath
The goodly fields, that earst so gay were dyde
In colours divers, quite despoyled hath,
All comfortlesse doth hide her chearlesse head
During the time of that her widowhead:

So we, that earst were wont in sweet accord
All places with our pleasant notes to fill,
Whilest favourable times did us afford
Free libertie to chaunt our charmes at will,
All comfortlesse upon the bared bow,
Like wofull culvers, doo sit wayling now.

For far more bitter storme than winters stowre
The beautie of the world hath lately wasted,
And those fresh buds, which wont so faire to flowre,
Hath marred quite, and all their blossoms blasted:
And those yong plants, which wont with fruit t' abound,
Now without fruite or leaves are to be found.

A stonie coldnesse hath benumbd the sence
And livelie spirits of each living wight,
And dimd with darknesse their intelligence,
Darknesse more than Cymerians daylie night:
And monstrous Error, flying in the ayre,
Hath mard the face of all that semed fayre.

Image of hellish horrour, Ignorance,
Borne in the bosome of the black abysse,
And fed with Furies milke, for sustenaunce
Of his weake infancie, begot amisse
By yawning Sloth on his owne mother Night;
So hee his sonnes both syre and brother hight:

He, armd with blindnesse and with boldnes stout,
(For blind is bold) hath our fayre light defaced;
And gathering unto him a ragged rout
Of faunes and satyres, hath our dwellings raced,
And our chast bowers, in which all vertue rained,
With brutishnesse and beastlie filth hath stained.

The sacred springs of horsefoot Helicon,
So oft bedeawed with our learned layes,
And speaking streames of pure Castalion,
The famous witnesse of our wonted praise,
They trampled have with their fowle footings trade,
And like to troubled puddles have them made.

Our pleasant groves, which planted were with paines,

That with our musick wont so oft to ring,
And arbors sweet, in which the shepheards swaines
Were wont so oft their pastoralls to sing,
They have cut downe, and all their pleasaunce mard,
That now no pastorall is to bee hard.

In stead of them, fowle goblins and shriekowles
With fearfull howling do all places fill;
And feeble Eccho now laments and howles,
The dreadfull accents of their outcries shrill.
So all is turned into wildernesse,
Whilest Ignorance the Muses doth oppresse.

And I, whose joy was earst with spirit full
To teach the warbling pipe to sound aloft,
My spirits now dismayd with sorrow dull,
Doo mone my miserie in silence soft.
Therefore I mourne and waile incessantly,
Till please the heavens affoord me remedy.

Therewith shee wayled with exceeding woe,
And pitious lamentation did make,
And all her sisters, seeing her doo soe,
With equall plaints her sorrowe did partake.
So rested shee: and then the next in rew
Began her grievous plaint, as doth ensew.

TERPSICHORE.
Who so hath in the lap of soft delight
Beene long time luld, and fed with pleasures sweet,
Feareles through his own fault or Fortunes spight,
To tumble into sorrow and regreet,
Yf chaunce him fall into calamitie,
Findes greater burthen of his miserie.

So wee, that earst in joyance did abound,
And in the bosome of all blis did sit,
Like virgin queenes with laurell garlands cround,
For vertues meed and ornament of wit,
Sith Ignorance our kingdome did confound,
Bee now become most wretched wightes on ground.

And in our royall thrones, which lately stood
In th' hearts of men to rule them carefully,
He now hath placed his accursed brood,
By him begotten of fowle Infamy;
Blind Error, scornefull Follie, and base Spight,
Who hold by wrong that wee should have by right.

They to the vulgar sort now pipe and sing,
And make them merrie with their fooleries;

They cherelie chaunt and rymes at randon fling,
The fruitfull spawne of their ranke fantasies;
They feede the eares of fooles with flattery,
And good men blame, and losels magnify.

All places they doo with their toyes possesse,
And raigne in liking of the multitude;
The schooles they fill with fond newfanglenesse,
And sway in court with pride and rashnes rude;
Mongst simple shepheards they do boast their skill,
And say their musicke matcheth Phœbus quill.

The noble hearts to pleasures they allure,
And tell their Prince that learning is but vaine;
Faire ladies loves they spot with thoughts impure,
And gentle mindes with lewd delights distaine;
Clerks they to loathly idlenes entice,
And fill their bookes with discipline of vice.

So every where they rule and tyrannize,
For their usurped kingdomes maintenaunce,
The whiles we silly maides, whom they dispize
And with reprochfull scorne discountenaunce,
From our owne native heritage exilde,
Walk through the world of every one revilde.

Nor anie one doth care to call us in,
Or once vouchsafeth us to entertaine,
Unlesse some one perhaps of gentle kin,
For pitties sake, compassion our paine,
And yeeld us some reliefe in this distresse;
Yet to be so reliev'd is wretchednesse.

So wander we all carefull comfortlesse,
Yet none doth care to comfort us at all;
So seeke we helpe our sorrow to redresse,
Yet none vouchsafes to answere to our call:
Therefore we mourne and pittilesse complaine,
Because none living pittieth our paine.

With that she wept and wofullie waymented,
That naught on earth her griefe might pacifie;
And all the rest her dolefull din augmented
With shrikes and groanes and grievous agonie.
So ended shee: and then the next in rew
Began her piteous plaint, as doth ensew.

ERATO.
Ye gentle spirits breathing from above,
Where ye in Venus silver bowre were bred,
Thoughts halfe devine, full of the fire of love,

With beawtie kindled and with pleasure fed,
Which ye now in securitie possesse,
Forgetfull of your former heavinesse:

Now change the tenor of your joyous layes,
With which ye use your loves to deifie,
And blazon foorth an earthlie beauties praise
Above the compasse of the arched skie:
Now change your praises into piteous cries,
And eulogies turne into elegies.

Such as ye wont, whenas those bitter stounds
Of raging love first gan you to torment,
And launch your hearts with lamentable wounds
Of secret sorrow and sad languishment,
Before your loves did take you unto grace;
Those now renew, as fitter for this place.

For I that rule in measure moderate
The tempest of that stormie passion,
And use to paint in rimes the troublous state
Of lovers life in likest fashion,
Am put from practise of my kindlie skill,
Banisht by those that love with leawdnes fill.

Love wont to be schoolmaster of my skill,
And the devicefull matter of my song;
Sweete love devoyd of villanie or ill,
But pure and spotles, as at first he sprong
Out of th' Almighties bosome, where he nests;
From thence infused into mortall brests.

Such high conceipt of that celestiall fire,
The base-borne brood of Blindnes cannot gesse,
Ne ever dare their dunghill thoughts aspire
Unto so loftie pitch of perfectnesse,
But rime at riot, and doo rage in love;
Yet little wote what doth thereto behove.

Faire Cytheree, the mother of delight
And queene of beautie, now thou maist go pack;
For lo! thy kingdome is defaced quight,
Thy scepter rent, and power put to wrack;
And thy gay sonne, that winged God of Love,
May now goe prune his plumes like ruffed dove.

And ye three twins, to light by Venus brought,
The sweete companions of the Muses late,
From whom what ever thing is goodly thought
Doth borrow grace, the fancie to aggrate,
Go beg with us, and be companions still,

As heretofore of good, so now of ill.

For neither you nor we shall anie more
Finde entertainment, or in court or schoole:
For that which was accounted heretofore
The learneds meed is now lent to the foole;
He sings of love, and maketh loving layes,
And they him heare, and they him highly prayse.

With that she powred foorth a brackish flood
Of bitter teares, and made exceeding mone;
And all her sisters, seeing her sad mood,
With lowd laments her answered all at one.
So ended she: and then the next in rew
Began her grievous plaint, as doth ensew.

CALLIOPE.
To whom shall I my evill case complaine,
Or tell the anguish of my inward smart,
Sith none is left to remedie my paine,
Or deignes to pitie a perplexed hart;
But rather seekes my sorrow to augment
With fowle reproach, and cruell banishment?

For they to whom I used to applie
The faithfull service of my learned skill,
The goodly off-spring of Joves progenie,
That wont the world with famous acts to fill;
Whose living praises in heroïck style,
It is my chiefe profession to compyle;

They all corrupted through the rust of time,
That doth all fairest things on earth deface,
Or through unnoble sloth, or sinfull crime,
That doth degenerate the noble race,
Have both desire of worthie deeds forlorne,
And name of learning utterly doo scorne.

Ne doo they care to have the auncestrie
Of th' old heroës memorizde anew;
Ne doo they care that late posteritie
Should know their names, or speak their praises dew:
But die forgot from whence at first they sprong,
As they themselves shalbe forgot ere long.

What bootes it then to come from glorious
Forefathers, or to have been nobly bredd?
What oddes twixt Irus and old Inachus,
Twixt best and worst, when both alike are dedd,
If none of neither mention should make,
Nor out of dust their memories awake?

Or who would ever care to doo brave deed,
Or strive in vertue others to excell,
If none should yeeld him his deserved meed,
Due praise, that is the spur of dooing well?
For if good were not praised more than ill,
None would choose goodnes of his owne freewill.

Therefore the nurse of vertue I am hight,
And golden trompet of eternitie,
That lowly thoughts lift up to heavens hight,
And mortall men have powre to deifie:
Bacchus and Hercules I raised to heaven,
And Charlemaine, amongst the starris seaven.

But now I will my golden clarion rend,
And will henceforth immortalize no more,
Sith I no more finde worthie to commend
For prize of value, or for learned lore:
For noble peeres, whom I was wont to raise,
Now onely seeke for pleasure, nought for praise.

Their great revenues all in sumptuous pride
They spend, that nought to learning they may spare;
And the rich fee which poets wont divide
Now parasites and sycophants doo share:
Therefore I mourne and endlesse sorrow make,
Both for my selfe and for my sisters sake.

With that she lowdly gan to waile and shrike,
And from her eyes a sea of teares did powre,
And all her sisters, with compassion like,
Did more increase the sharpnes of her showre.
So ended she: and then the next in rew
Began her plaint, as doth herein ensew.

URANIA.
What wrath of gods, or wicked influence
Of starres conspiring wretched men t' afflict,
Hath powrd on earth this noyous pestilence,
That mortall mindes doth inwardly infect
With love of blindnesse and of ignorance,
To dwell in darkenesse without sovenance?

What difference twixt man and beast is left,
When th' heavenlie light of knowledge is put out,
And th' ornaments of wisdome are bereft?
Then wandreth he in error and in doubt,
Unweeting of the danger hee is in,
Through fleshes frailtie and deceipt of sin.

In this wide world in which they wretches stray,
It is the onelie comfort which they have,
It is their light, their loadstarre and their day;
But hell and darkenesse and the grislie grave
Is ignorance, the enemie of grace,
That mindes of men borne heavenlie doth debace.

Through knowledge we behold the worlds creation,
How in his cradle first he fostred was;
And judge of Natures cunning operation,
How things she formed of a formelesse mas:
By knowledge wee do learne our selves to knowe,
And what to man, and what to God, wee owe.

From hence wee mount aloft unto the skie,
And looke into the christall firmament;
There we behold the heavens great hierarchie,
The starres pure light, the spheres swift movement,
The spirites and intelligences fayre,
And angels waighting on th' Almighties chayre.

And there, with humble minde and high insight,
Th' eternall Makers majestie wee viewe,
His love, his truth, his glorie, and his might,
And mercie more than mortall men can vew.
O soveraigne Lord, O soveraigne happinesse,
To see thee, and thy mercie measurelesse!

Such happines have they that doo embrace
The precepts of my heavenlie discipline;
But shame and sorrow and accursed case
Have they that scorne the schoole of arts divine,
And banish me, which do professe the skill
To make men heavenly wise through humbled will.

How ever yet they mee despise and spight,
I feede on sweet contentment of my thought,
And please my selfe with mine owne selfe-delight,
In contemplation of things heavenlie wrought:
So loathing earth, I looke up to the sky,
And being driven hence, I thether fly.

Thence I behold the miserie of men,
Which want the blis that wisedom would them breed,
And like brute beasts doo lie in loathsome den
Of ghostly darkenes, and of gastlie dreed:
For whom I mourne, and for my selfe complaine,
And for my sisters eake, whom they disdaine.

With that shee wept and waild so pityouslie,
As if her eyes had beene two springing wells:

And all the rest, her sorrow to supplie,
Did throw forth shrieks and cries and dreery yells.
So ended shee: and then the next in rew
Began her mournfull plaint, as doth ensew.

POLYHYMNIA.
A dolefull case desires a dolefull song,
Without vaine art or curious complements,
And squallid fortune, into basenes flong,
Doth scorne the pride of wonted ornaments.
Then fittest are these ragged rimes for mee,
To tell my sorrowes that exceeding bee.

For the sweet numbers and melodious measures,
With which I wont the winged words to tie,
And make a tunefull diapase of pleasures,
Now being let to runne at libertie
By those which have no skill to rule them right,
Have now quite lost their naturall delight.

Heapes of huge words uphoorded hideously,
With horrid sound, though having little sence,
They thinke to be chiefe praise of poëtry;
And thereby wanting due intelligence,
Have mard the face of goodly poësie,
And made a monster of their fantasie.

Whilom in ages past none might professe,
But princes and high priests, that secret skill;
The sacred lawes therein they wont expresse,
And with deepe oracles their verses fill:
Then was shee held in soveraigne dignitie,
And made the noursling of nobilitie.

But now nor prince nor priest doth her maintayne,
But suffer her prophaned for to bee
Of the base vulgar, that with hands uncleane
Dares to pollute her hidden mysterie;
And treadeth under foote hir holie things,
Which was the care of kesars and of kings.

One onelie lives, her ages ornament,
And myrrour of her Makers majestie;
That with rich bountie and deare cherishment
Supports the praise of noble poësie:
Ne onelie favours them which it professe,
But is her selfe a peereles poëtresse.

Most peereles prince, most peereles poëtresse,
The true Pandora of all heavenly graces,
Divine Elisa, sacred Emperesse:

Live she for ever, and her royall p'laces
Be fild with praises of divinest wits,
That her eternize with their heavenlie writs.

Some few beside this sacred skill esteme,
Admirers of her glorious excellence,
Which being lightned with her beawties beme,
Are thereby fild with happie influence,
And lifted up above the worldes gaze,
To sing with angels her immortall praize.

But all the rest, as borne of salvage brood,
And having beene with acorns alwaies fed,
Can no whit savour this celestiall food,
But with base thoughts are into blindnesse led,
And kept from looking on the lightsome day:
For whome I waile and weepe all that I may.

Eftsoones such store of teares shee forth did powre,
As if shee all to water would have gone;
And all her sisters, seeing her sad stowre,
Did weep and waile and made exceeding mone;
And all their learned instruments did breake:
The rest untold no living tongue can speake.

FINIS.

VIRGILS GNAT - LONG SINCE DEDICATED TO THE MOST NOBLE AND EXCELLENT LORD, THE EARLE
OF LEICESTER, LATE DECEASED

Wrong'd, yet not daring to expresse my paine,
To you (great Lord) the causer of my care,
In clowdie teares my ease I thus complaine
Unto your selfe, that onely privie are:
But if that any Œdipus unware
Shall chaunce, through power of some divining spright,
To reade the secrete of this riddle rare,
And know the purporte of my evill plight,
Let him rest pleased with his owne insight,
Ne further seeke to glose upon the text:
For griefe enough it is to grieved wight
To feele his fault, and not be further vext.
But what so by my selfe may not be showen,
May by this Gnatts complaint be easily knowen.

Virgil's Gnat' may be thought to follow close upon the latest of the sonnet series. The main period to
which it belongs is, in any case, certain, for in the title it is described as 'long since dedicated' to the

Earl of Leicester; it deals with some mishap in the personal relations of the poet with that nobleman, and such relations would seem to have been confined to the years 1577-1580. What the mishap may have been has remained, on the other hand, obscure. The curious must divine it as they best may from the sonnet of dedication and from the main allegory, always remembering that the poem is not an invention based upon the circumstances, but a mere paraphrase of the pseudo-Virgilian Culex. Of greater moment is the style, which, moving in a freer course than is natural to the sonnet, wins nearer than that of the 'Visions' and 'Ruins of Rome' to the cadences of the Faery Queen. The use of ottava rima, the stanza of the great Italian romances, points forward, too.

VIRGILS GNAT

We now have playde (Augustus) wantonly,
Tuning our song unto a tender Muse,
And like a cobweb weaving slenderly,
Have onely playde: let thus much then excuse
This Gnats small poeme, that th' whole history
Is but a jest, though envie it abuse:
But who such sports and sweet delights doth blame,
Shall lighter seeme than this Gnats idle name.

Hereafter, when as season more secure
Shall bring forth fruit, this Muse shall speak to thee
In bigger notes, that may thy sense allure,
And for thy worth frame some fit poesie:
The golden ofspring of Latona pure,
And ornament of great Joves progenie,
Phœbus, shall be the author of my song,
Playing on yvorie harp with silver strong.

He shall inspire my verse with gentle mood,
Of poets prince, whether he woon beside
Faire Xanthus sprincled with Chimæras blood,
Or in the woods of Astery abide,
Or whereas Mount Parnasse, the Muses brood,
Doth his broad forhead like two hornes divide,
And the sweete waves of sounding Castaly
With liquid foote doth slide downe easily.

Wherefore ye sisters, which the glorie bee
Of the Pierian streames, fayre Naiades,
Go too, and dauncing all in companie,
Adorne that god: and thou holie Pales,
To whome the honest care of husbandrie
Returneth by continuall successe,
Have care for to pursue his footing light,
Through the wide woods and groves with green leaves dight.

Professing thee I lifted am aloft
Betwixt the forrest wide and starrie sky:

And thou most dread (Octavius) which oft
To learned wits givest courage worthily,
O come (thou sacred childe) come sliding soft,
And favour my beginnings graciously:
For not these leaves do sing that dreadfull stound,
When giants bloud did staine Phlegræan ground;

Nor how th' halfe horsy people, Centaures hight,
Fought with the bloudie Lapithaes at bord;
Nor how the East with tyranous despight
Burnt th' Attick towres, and people slew with sword;
Nor how Mount Athos through exceeding might
Was digged downe; nor yron bands abord
The Pontick sea by their huge navy cast,
My volume shall renowne, so long since past:

Nor Hellespont trampled with horses feete,
When flocking Persians did the Greeks affray;
But my soft Muse, as for her power more meete,
Delights (with Phœbus friendly leave) to play
An easie running verse with tender feete.
And thou (dread sacred child) to thee alway
Let everlasting lightsome glory strive,
Through the worlds endles ages to survive.

And let an happie roome remaine for thee
Mongst heavenly ranks, where blessed soules do rest;
And let long lasting life with joyous glee,
As thy due meede that thou deservest best,
Hereafter many yeares remembred be
Amongst good men, of whom thou oft are blest;
Live thou for ever in all happinesse:
But let us turne to our first businesse.

The fiery Sun was mounted now on hight
Up to the heavenly towers, and shot each where
Out of his golden charet glistering light;
And fayre Aurora with her rosie heare
The hatefull darknes now had put to flight;
When as the shepheard, seeing day appeare,
His little goats gan drive out of their stalls,
To feede abroad, where pasture best befalls.

To an high mountaines top he with them went,
Where thickest grasse did cloath the open hills:
They, now amongst the woods and thickets ment,
Now in the valleies wandring at their wills,
Spread themselves farre abroad through each descent;
Some on the soft greene grasse feeding their fills;
Some, clambring through the hollow cliffes on hy,
Nibble the bushie shrubs, which growe thereby.

Others the utmost boughs of trees doe crop,
And brouze the woodbine twigges, that freshly bud;
This with full bit doth catch the utmost top
Of some soft willow, or new growen stud;
This with sharpe teeth the bramble leaves doth lop,
And chaw the tender prickles in her cud;
The whiles another high doth overlooke
Her owne like image in a christall brooke.

O the great happines which shepheards have,
Who so loathes not too much the poore estate
With minde that ill use doth before deprave,
Ne measures all things by the costly rate
Of riotise, and semblants outward brave!
No such sad cares, as wont to macerate
And rend the greedie mindes of covetous men,
Do ever creepe into the shepheards den.

Ne cares he if the fleece which him arayes
Be not twice steeped in Assyrian dye;
Ne glistering of golde, which underlayes
The summer beames, doe blinde his gazing eye;
Ne pictures beautie, nor the glauncing rayes
Of precious stones, whence no good commeth by;
Ne yet his cup embost with imagery
Of Bætus or of Alcons vanity.

Ne ought the whelky pearles esteemeth hee,
Which are from Indian seas brought far away:
But with pure brest from carefull sorrow free,
On the soft grasse his limbs doth oft display,
In sweete spring time, when flowres varietie
With sundrie colours paints the sprincled lay;
There, lying all at ease from guile or spight,
With pype of fennie reedes doth him delight.

There he, lord of himselfe, with palme bedight,
His looser locks doth wrap in wreath of vine:
There his milk dropping goats be his delight,
And fruitefull Pales, and the forrest greene,
And darkesome caves in pleasaunt vallies pight,
Wheras continuall shade is to be seene,
And where fresh springing wells, as christall neate,
Do alwayes flow, to quench his thirstie heate.

O who can lead then a more happie life
Than he, that with cleane minde and heart sincere,
No greedy riches knowes nor bloudie strife,
No deadly fight of warlick fleete doth feare,
Ne runs in perill of foes cruell knife,

That in the sacred temples he may reare
A trophee of his glittering spoyles and treasure,
Or may abound in riches above measure?

Of him his God is worshipt with his sythe,
And not with skill of craftsman polished:
He joyes in groves, and makes himselfe full blythe
With sundrie flowers in wilde fieldes gathered;
Ne frankincens he from Panchæa buyth:
Sweete Quiet harbours in his harmeles head,
And perfect Pleasure buildes her joyous bowre,
Free from sad cares, that rich mens hearts devowre.

This all his care, this all his whole indevour,
To this his minde and senses he doth bend,
How he may flow in quiets matchles treasour,
Content with any food that God doth send;
And how his limbs, resolv'd through idle leisour
Unto sweete sleepe he may securely lend,
In some coole shadow from the scorching heat,
The whiles his flock their chawed cuds do eate.

O flocks, O faunes, and O ye pleasaunt springs
Of Tempe, where the countrey nymphs are rife,
Through whose not costly care each shepheard sings
As merrie notes upon his rusticke fife
As that Ascræan bard, whose fame now rings
Through the wide world, and leads as joyfull life,
Free from all troubles and from worldly toyle,
In which fond men doe all their dayes turmoyle.

In such delights whilst thus his carelesse time
This shepheard drives, upleaning on his batt,
And on shrill reedes chaunting his rustick rime,
Hyperion, throwing foorth his beames full hott,
Into the highest top of heaven gan clime,
And the world parting by an equall lott,
Did shed his whirling flames on either side,
As the great Ocean doth himselfe divide.

Then gan the shepheard gather into one
His stragling goates, and drave them to a foord,
Whose cærule streame, rombling in pible stone,
Crept under mosse as greene as any goord.
Now had the sun halfe heaven overgone,
When he his heard back from that water foord
Drave from the force of Phœbus boyling ray,
Into thick shadowes, there themselves to lay.

Soone as he them plac'd in thy sacred wood
(O Delian goddesse) saw, to which of yore

Came the bad daughter of old Cadmus brood,
Cruell Agave, flying vengeance sore
Of King Nictileus for the guiltie blood
Which she with cursed hands had shed before;
There she halfe frantick having slaine her sonne,
Did shrowd her selfe like punishment to shonne.

Here also playing on the grassy greene,
Woodgods, and satyres, and swift dryades,
With many fairies oft were dauncing seene.
Not so much did Dan Orpheus represse
The streames of Hebrus with his songs, I weene,
As that faire troupe of woodie goddesses
Staied thee (O Peneus) powring foorth to thee,
From cheereful lookes, great mirth and gladsome glee.

The verie nature of the place, resounding
With gentle murmure of the breathing ayre,
A pleasant bowre with all delight abounding
In the fresh shadowe did for them prepayre,
To rest their limbs with wearines redounding.
For first the high palme trees, with braunches faire,
Out of the lowly vallies did arise,
And high shoote up their heads into the skyes.

And them amongst the wicked lotos grew,
Wicked, for holding guilefully away
Ulysses men, whom rapt with sweetenes new,
Taking to hoste, it quite from him did stay;
And eke those trees, in whose transformed hew
The Sunnes sad daughters waylde the rash decay
Of Phaeton, whose limbs with lightening rent
They gathering up, with sweete teares did lament.

And that same tree, in which Demophoon,
By his disloyalty lamented sore,
Eternall hurte left unto many one:
Whom als accompanied the oke, of yore
Through fatall charmes transformd to such an one:
The oke, whose acornes were our foode, before
That Ceres seede of mortall men were knowne,
Which first Triptoleme taught how to be sowne.

Here also grew the rougher rinded pine,
The great Argoan ships brave ornament,
Whom golden fleece did make an heavenly signe;
Which coveting, with his high tops extent,
To make the mountaines touch the starres divine,
Decks all the forrest with embellishment;
And the blacke holme that loves the watrie vale;
And the sweete cypresse, signe of deadly bale.

Emongst the rest the clambring yvie grew,
Knitting his wanton armes with grasping hold,
Least that the poplar happely should rew
Her brothers strokes, whose boughes she doth enfold
With her lythe twigs, till they the top survew,
And paint with pallid greene her buds of gold.
Next did the myrtle tree to her approach,
Not yet unmindfull of her olde reproach.

But the small birds, in their wide boughs embowring,
Chaunted their sundrie tunes with sweete consent;
And under them a silver spring, forth powring
His trickling streames, a gentle murmure sent;
Thereto the frogs, bred in the slimie scowring
Of the moist moores, their jarring voyces bent;
And shrill grashoppers chirped them around:
All which the ayrie echo did resound.

In this so pleasant place this shepheards flocke
Lay everie where, their wearie limbs to rest,
On everie bush, and everie hollow rocke,
Where breathe on them the whistling wind mote best;
The whiles the shepheard self, tending his stocke,
Sate by the fountaine side, in shade to rest,
Where gentle slumbring sleep oppressed him,
Displaid on ground, and seized everie lim.

Of trecherie or traines nought tooke he keep,
But, looslie on the grassie greene dispredd,
His dearest life did trust to careles sleep;
Which, weighing down his drouping drowsie hedd,
In quiet rest his molten heart did steep,
Devoid of care, and feare of all falshedd:
Had not inconstant Fortune, bent to ill,
Bid strange mischance his quietnes to spill.

For at his wonted time in that same place
An huge great serpent, all with speckles pide,
To drench himselfe in moorish slime did trace,
There from the boyling heate himselfe to hide:
He, passing by with rolling wreathed pace,
With brandisht tongue the emptie aire did gride,
And wrapt his scalie boughts with fell despight,
That all things seem'd appalled at his sight.

Now more and more having himselfe enrolde,
His glittering breast he lifteth up on hie,
And with proud vaunt his head aloft doth holde;
His creste above, spotted with purple die,
On everie side did shine like scalie golde,

And his bright eyes, glauncing full dreadfullie,
Did seeme to flame out flakes of flashing fyre,
And with sterne lookes to threaten kindled yre.

Thus wise long time he did himselfe dispace
There round about, when as at last he spide,
Lying along before him in that place,
That flocks grand captaine and most trustie guide:
Eftsoones more fierce in visage and in pace,
Throwing his firie eyes on everie side,
He commeth on, and all things in his way
Full stearnly rends, that might his passage stay.

Much he disdaines, that anie one should dare
To come unto his haunt; for which intent
He inly burns, and gins straight to prepare
The weapons which Nature to him hath lent;
Fellie he hisseth, and doth fiercely stare,
And hath his jawes with angrie spirits rent,
That all his tract with bloudie drops is stained,
And all his foldes are now in length outstrained.

Whom, thus at point prepared, to prevent,
A litle noursling of the humid ayre,
A Gnat, unto the sleepie shepheard went,
And marking where his ey-lids, twinckling rare,
Shewd the two pearles which sight unto him lent,
Through their thin coverings appearing fayre,
His little needle there infixing deep,
Warnd him awake, from death himselfe to keep.

Wherewith enrag'd, he fiercely gan upstart,
And with his hand him rashly bruzing, slewe,
As in avengement of his heedles smart,
That streight the spirite out of his senses flew,
And life out of his members did depart:
When suddenly casting aside his vew,
He spide his foe with felonous intent,
And fervent eyes to his destruction bent.

All suddenly dismaid, and hartles quight,
He fled abacke, and, catching hastie holde
Of a yong alder hard beside him pight,
It rent, and streight about him gan beholde
What god or fortune would assist his might.
But whether god or fortune made him bold
Its hard to read: yet hardie will he had
To overcome, that made him lesse adrad.

The scalie backe of that most hideous snake
Enwrapped round, oft faining to retire,

And oft him to assaile, he fiercely strake
Whereas his temples did his creast front tyre;
And, for he was but slowe, did slowth off shake,
And gazing ghastly on (for feare and yre
Had blent so much his sense, that lesse he feard;)
Yet, when he saw him slaine, himselfe he cheard.

By this the Night forth from the darksome bowre
Of Herebus her teemed steedes gan call,
And laesie Vesper in his timely howre
From golden Oeta gan proceede withall;
Whenas the shepheard after this sharpe stowre,
Seing the doubled shadowes low to fall,
Gathering his straying flocke, does homeward fare,
And unto rest his wearie joynts prepare.

Into whose sense so soone as lighter sleepe
Was entered, and now loosing everie lim,
Sweete slumbring deaw in carelesnesse did steepe,
The image of that Gnat appeard to him,
And in sad tearmes gan sorrowfully weepe,
With greislie countenaunce and visage grim,
Wailing the wrong which he had done of late,
In steed of good, hastning his cruell fate.

Said he, 'What have I, wretch, deserv'd, that thus
Into this bitter bale I am outcast,
Whilest that thy life more deare and precious
Was than mine owne, so long as it did last?
I now, in lieu of paines so gracious,
Am tost in th' ayre with everie windie blast:
Thou, safe delivered from sad decay,
Thy careles limbs in loose sleep dost display.

'So livest thou; but my poore wretched ghost
Is forst to ferrie over Lethes river,
And, spoyld of Charon, too and fro am tost.
Seest thou, how all places quake and quiver,
Lightned with deadly lamps on everie post?
Tisiphone each where doth shake and shiver
Her flaming fire brond, encountring me,
Whose lockes uncombed cruell adders be.

'And Cerberus, whose many mouthes doo bay,
And barke out flames, as if on fire he fed;
Adowne whose necke, in terrible array,
Ten thousand snakes, cralling about his hed,
Doo hang in heapes, that horribly affray,
And bloodie eyes doo glister firie red;
He oftentimes me dreadfullie doth threaten,
With painfull torments to be sorely beaten.

'Ay me! that thankes so much should faile of meed!
For that I thee restor'd to life againe,
Even from the doore of death and deadlie dreed.
Where then is now the guerdon of my paine?
Where the reward of my so piteous deed?
The praise of pitie vanisht is in vaine,
And th' antique faith of justice long agone
Out of the land is fled away and gone.

'I saw anothers fate approaching fast,
And left mine owne his safetie to tender;
Into the same mishap I now am cast,
And shun'd destruction doth destruction render:
Not unto him that never hath trespast,
But punishment is due to the offender:
Yet let destruction be the punishment,
So long as thankfull will may it relent.

'I carried am into waste wildernesse,
Waste wildernes, amongst Cymerian shades,
Where endles paines and hideous heavinesse
Is round about me heapt in darksome glades.
For there huge Othos sits in sad distresse,
Fast bound with serpents that him oft invades,
Far of beholding Ephialtes tide,
Which once assai'd to burne this world so wide.

'And there is mournfull Tityus, mindefull yet
Of thy displeasure, O Latona faire;
Displeasure too implacable was it,
That made him meat for wild foules of the ayre:
Much do I feare among such fiends to sit;
Much do I feare back to them to repayre,
To the black shadowes of the Stygian shore,
Where wretched ghosts sit wailing evermore.

'There next the utmost brinck doth he abide,
That did the bankets of the gods bewray,
Whose throat, through thirst, to nought nigh being dride,
His sense to seeke for ease turnes every way:
And he that in avengement of his pride,
For scorning to the sacred gods to pray,
Against a mountaine rolls a mightie stone,
Calling in vaine for rest, and can have none.

'Go ye with them, go, cursed damosells,
Whose bridale torches foule Erynnis tynde,
And Hymen, at your spousalls sad, foretells
Tydings of death and massacre unkinde:
With them that cruell Colchid mother dwells,

The which conceiv'd in her revengefull minde,
With bitter woundes her owne deere babes to slay,
And murdred troupes upon great heapes to lay.

'There also those two Pandionian maides,
Calling on Itis, Itis evermore,
Whom, wretched boy, they slew with guiltie blades;
For whome the Thracian king lamenting sore,
Turn'd to a lapwing, fowlie them upbraydes,
And fluttering round about them still does sore;
There now they all eternally complaine
Of others wrong, and suffer endles paine.

'But the two brethren borne of Cadmus blood,
Whilst each does for the soveraignty contend,
Blinde through ambition, and with vengeance wood,
Each doth against the others bodie bend
His cursed steele, of neither well withstood,
And with wide wounds their carcases doth rend;
That yet they both doe mortall foes remaine,
Sith each with brothers bloudie hand was slaine.

'Ah (waladay!) there is no end of paine,
Nor chaunge of labour may intreated bee:
Yet I beyond all these am carried faine,
Where other powers farre different I see,
And must passe over to th' Elisian plaine:
There grim Persephone, encountring mee,
Doth urge her fellow Furies earnestlie,
With their bright firebronds me to terrifie.

'There chast Alceste lives inviolate,
Free from all care, for that her husbands daies
She did prolong by changing fate for fate:
Lo! there lives also the immortall praise
Of womankinde, most faithfull to her mate,
Penelope; and from her farre awayes
A rulesse rout of youngmen, which her woo'd,
All slaine with darts, lie wallowed in their blood.

'And sad Eurydice thence now no more
Must turne to life, but there detained bee,
For looking back, being forbid before:
Yet was the guilt thereof, Orpheus, in thee.
Bold sure he was, and worthie spirite bore,
That durst those lowest shadowes goe to see,
And could beleeve that anie thing could please
Fell Cerberus, or Stygian powres appease.

'Ne feard the burning waves of Phlegeton,
Nor those same mournfull kingdomes, compassed

With rustie horrour and fowle fashion,
And deep digd vawtes, and Tartar covered
With bloodie night, and darke confusion,
And judgement seates, whose judge is deadlie dred,
A judge that, after death, doth punish sore
The faults which life hath trespassed before.

'But valiant fortune made Dan Orpheus bolde:
For the swift running rivers still did stand,
And the wilde beasts their furie did withhold,
To follow Orpheus musicke through the land:
And th' okes, deep grounded in the earthly molde,
Did move, as if they could him understand;
And the shrill woods, which were of sense bereav'd,
Through their hard barke his silver sound receav'd.

'And eke the Moone her hastie steedes did stay,
Drawing in teemes along the starrie skie;
And didst (O monthly virgin) thou delay
Thy nightly course, to heare his melodie?
The same was able, with like lovely lay,
The Queene of Hell to move as easily,
To yeeld Eurydice unto her fere,
Backe to be borne, though it unlawfull were.

'She (ladie) having well before approoved,
The feends to be too cruell and severe,
Observ'd th' appointed way, as her behooved,
Ne ever did her ey-sight turne arere,
Ne ever spake, ne cause of speaking mooved:
But cruell Orpheus, thou much crueller,
Seeking to kisse her, brok'st the gods decree,
And thereby mad'st her ever damn'd to be.

'Ah! but sweete love of pardon worthie is,
And doth deserve to have small faults remitted;
If Hell at least things lightly done amis
Knew how to pardon, when ought is omitted:
Yet are ye both received into blis,
And to the seates of happie soules admitted,
And you beside the honourable band
Of great heroës doo in order stand.

'There be the two stout sonnes of Aeacus,
Fierce Peleus, and the hardie Telamon,
Both seeming now full glad and joyeous
Through their syres dreadfull jurisdiction,
Being the judge of all that horrid hous:
And both of them, by strange occasion,
Renown'd in choyce of happie marriage
Through Venus grace, and vertues cariage.

'For th' one was ravisht of his owne bondmaide,
The faire Ixione, captiv'd from Troy;
But th' other was with Thetis love assaid,
Great Nereus his daughter and his joy.
On this side them there is a youngman layd,
Their match in glorie, mightie, fierce and coy,
That from th' Argolick ships, with furious yre,
Bett back the furie of the Trojan fyre.

'O who would not recount the strong divorces
Of that great warre, which Trojanes oft behelde,
And oft beheld the warlike Greekish forces,
When Teucrian soyle with bloodie rivers swelde,
And wide Sigæan shores were spred with corses,
And Simois and Xanthus blood outwelde,
Whilst Hector raged with outragious minde,
Flames, weapons, wounds in Greeks fleete to have tynde?

'For Ida selfe, in ayde of that fierce fight,
Out of her mountaines ministred supplies,
And like a kindly nourse, did yeeld (for spight)
Store of firebronds out of her nourseries
Unto her foster children, that they might
Inflame the navie of their enemies,
And all the Rhætean shore to ashes turne,
Where lay the ships which they did seeke to burne.

'Gainst which the noble sonne of Telamon
Opposd' himselfe, and thwarting his huge shield,
Them battell bad; gainst whom appeard anon
Hector, the glorie of the Trojan field:
Both fierce and furious in contention
Encountred, that their mightie strokes so shrild
As the great clap of thunder, which doth ryve
The ratling heavens, and cloudes asunder dryve.

'So th' one with fire and weapons did contend
To cut the ships from turning home againe
To Argos; th' other strove for to defend
The force of Vulcane with his might and maine.
Thus th' one Aeacide did his fame extend:
But th' other joy'd, that, on the Phrygian playne
Having the blood of vanquisht Hector shedd,
He compast Troy thrice with his bodie dedd.

'Againe great dole on either partie grewe,
That him to death unfaithfull Paris sent;
And also him that false Ulysses slewe,
Drawne into danger through close ambushment:
Therefore from him Laërtes sonne his vewe

Doth turne aside, and boasts his good event
In working of Strymonian Rhæsus fall,
And efte in Dolons slye surprysall.

'Againe the dreadfull Cycones him dismay,
And blacke Læstrigones, a people stout:
Then greedie Scilla, under whom there bay
Manie great bandogs, which her gird about:
Then doo the Aetnean Cyclops him affray,
And deep Charybdis gulphing in and out:
Lastly the squalid lakes of Tartarie,
And griesly feends of hell him terrifie.

'There also goodly Agamemnon bosts,
The glorie of the stock of Tantalus,
And famous light of all the Greekish hosts,
Under whose conduct most victorious,
The Dorick flames consum'd the Iliack posts.
Ah! but the Greekes themselves more dolorous,
To thee, O Troy, paid penaunce for thy fall,
In th' Hellespont being nigh drowned all.

'Well may appeare, by proofe of their mischaunce,
The chaungfull turning of mens slipperie state,
That none, whom fortune freely doth advaunce,
Himselfe therefore to heaven should elevate:
For loftie type of honour, through the glaunce
Of envies dart, is downe in dust prostrate;
And all that vaunts in worldly vanitie
Shall fall through fortunes mutabilitie.

'Th' Argolicke power returning home againe,
Enricht with spoyles of th' Ericthonian towre,
Did happie winde and weather entertaine,
And with good speed the fomie billowes scowre:
No signe of storme, no feare of future paine,
Which soone ensued them with heavie stowre.
Nereïs to the seas a token gave,
The whiles their crooked keeles the surges clave.

'Suddenly, whether through the gods decree,
Or haplesse rising of some froward starre,
The heavens on everie side enclowded bee:
Black stormes and fogs are blowen up from farre,
That now the pylote can no loadstarre see,
But skies and seas doo make most dreadfull warre;
The billowes striving to the heavens to reach,
And th' heavens striving them for to impeach.

'And, in avengement of their bold attempt,
Both sun and starres and all the heavenly powres

Conspire in one to wreake their rash contempt,
And downe on them to fall from highest towres:
The skie, in pieces seeming to be rent,
Throwes lightning forth, and haile, and harmful showres,
That death on everie side to them appeares,
In thousand formes, to worke more ghastly feares.

'Some in the greedie flouds are sunke and drent;
Some on the rocks of Caphareus are throwne;
Some on th' Euboick cliffs in pieces rent;
Some scattred on the Hercæan shores unknowne;
And manie lost, of whom no moniment
Remaines, nor memorie is to be showne:
Whilst all the purchase of the Phrigian pray,
Tost on salt billowes, round about doth stray.

'Here manie other like heroës bee,
Equall in honour to the former crue,
Whom ye in goodly seates may placed see,
Descended all from Rome by linage due,
From Rome, that holds the world in sovereigntie,
And doth all nations unto her subdue:
Here Fabii and Decii doo dwell,
Horatii that in vertue did excell.

'And here the antique fame of stout Camill
Doth ever live; and constant Curtius,
Who, stifly bent his vowed life to spill
For countreyes health, a gulph most hideous
Amidst the towne with his owne corps did fill,
T' appease the powers; and prudent Mutius,
Who in his flesh endur'd the scorching flame,
To daunt his foe by ensample of the same.

'And here wise Curius, companion
Of noble vertues, lives in endles rest;
And stout Flaminius, whose devotion
Taught him the fires scorn'd furie to detest;
And here the praise of either Scipion
Abides in highest place above the best,
To whom the ruin'd walls of Carthage vow'd,
Trembling their forces, sound their praises lowd.

'Live they for ever through their lasting praise:
But I, poore wretch, am forced to retourne
To the sad lakes, that Phœbus sunnie rayes
Doo never see, where soules doo alwaies mourne;
And by the wayling shores to waste my dayes,
Where Phlegeton with quenchles flames doth burne;
By which just Minos righteous soules doth sever
From wicked ones, to live in blisse for ever.

'Me therefore thus the cruell fiends of hell,
Girt with long snakes and thousand yron chaynes,
Through doome of that their cruell judge, compell,
With bitter torture and impatient paines,
Cause of my death and just complaint to tell.
For thou art he whom my poore ghost complaines
To be the author of her ill unwares,
That careles hear'st my intollerable cares.

'Them therefore as bequeathing to the winde,
I now depart, returning to thee never,
And leave this lamentable plaint behinde.
But doo thou haunt the soft downe rolling river,
And wilde greene woods, and fruitful pastures minde,
And let the flitting aire my vaine words sever.'
Thus having said, he heavily departed
With piteous crie, that anie would have smarted.

Now, when the sloathfull fit of lifes sweete rest
Had left the heavie shepheard, wondrous cares
His inly grieved minde full sore opprest;
That balefull sorrow he no longer beares
For that Gnats death, which deeply was imprest,
But bends what ever power his aged yeares
Him lent, yet being such as through their might
He lately slue his dreadfull foe in fight.

By that same river lurking under greene,
Eftsoones he gins to fashion forth a place,
And squaring it in compasse well beseene,
There plotteth out a tombe by measured space:
His yron headed spade tho making cleene,
To dig up sods out of the flowrie grasse,
His worke he shortly to good purpose brought,
Like as he had conceiv'd it in his thought.

An heape of earth he hoorded up on hie,
Enclosing it with banks on everie side,
And thereupon did raise full busily
A little mount, of greene turffs edifide;
And on the top of all, that passers by
Might it behold, the toomb he did provide
Of smoothest marble stone in order set,
That never might his luckie scape forget.

And round about he taught sweete flowres to growe,
The rose engrained in pure scarlet die,
The lilly fresh, and violet belowe,
The marigolde, and cherefull rosemarie,
The Spartan mirtle, whence sweet guml does flowe,

The purple hyacinthe, and fresh cost-marie,
And saffron, sought for in Cilician soyle,
And lawrell, th' ornament of Phœbus toyle:

Fresh rhododaphne, and the Sabine flowre,
Matching the wealth of th' auncient frank-incence,
And pallid yvie, building his owne bowre,
And box, yet mindfull of his olde offence,
Red amaranthus, lucklesse paramour,
Oxeye still greene, and bitter patience;
Ne wants there pale Narcisse, that, in a well
Seeing his beautie, in love with it fell.

And whatsoever other flowre of worth,
And whatso other hearb of lovely hew
The joyous Spring out of the ground brings forth,
To cloath her selfe in colours fresh and new,
He planted there, and reard a mount of earth,
In whose high front was writ as doth ensue:

To thee, small Gnat, in lieu of his life saved,
The Shepheard hath thy deaths record engraved.

FINIS.

PROSOPOPOIA OR MOTHER HUBBERDS TALE - DEDICATED TO THE RIGHT HONORABLE THE LADIE COMPTON AND MOUNTEGLE

TO THE RIGHT HONOURABLE, THE LADIE COMPTON AND MOUNTEGLE

Most faire and vertuous Ladie: having often sought opportunitie by some good meanes to make knowen to your Ladiship the humble affection and faithfull duetie which I have alwaies professed, and am bound to beare, to that house from whence yee spring, I have at length found occasion to remember the same, by making a simple present to you of these my idle labours; which having long sithens composed in the raw conceipt of my youth, I lately amongst other papers lighted upon, and was by others, which liked the same, mooved to set them foorth. Simple is the device, and the composition meane, yet carrieth some delight, even the rather because of the simplicitie and meannesse thus personated. The same I beseech your Ladiship take in good part, as a pledge of that profession which I have made to you, and keepe with you untill, with some other more worthie labour, I do redeeme it out of your hands, and discharge my utmost dutie. Till then, wishing your Ladiship all increase of honour and happinesse, I humblie take leave.
Your Ladiships ever
humbly,

Edmund Spenser

'Mother Hubberd's Tale' is of the same period with 'Virgil's Gnat.' In the dedicatory letter of 1591 it is said to have been 'long sithens composed in the raw conceipt of my youth,' and 'long sithens' is limited by the satire on court life to the years from 1577 to 1580. A probable glance at the disgrace of Leicester in 1579 (l. 628) may limit it still more. Yet beside this very reference is one, equally probable, to events of ten years later, and other such insertions may be found. It would appear, therefore, that when, during his second sojourn at court, Spenser 'lighted upon' this early poem and was 'mooved to set it foorth,' he to some extent revised and enlarged it.

The most obvious characteristic of 'Mother Hubberd's Tale' is the range of its satire. The career of the Ape and the Fox is a kind of rogues' progress through the three estates to the crown. They begin among the common people, rise from thence to the clergy and from thence to the court, among the nobility; in the end they cap the climax of their villainies by making themselves king and prime minister. The satire is mainly concentrated, to be sure, upon life at the court and the intrigues of those in power, topics of direct personal concern to Spenser, yet the poem as a whole does survey, however imperfectly and unsymmetrically, some of the main conditions of life in the nation at large. In this it harks back unmistakably to Piers Plowman. Though the satiric scope is of Langland, however, there is much in the style to suggest the vein of Chaucer, and the dramatis personœ and stage-setting are those of Reynard the Fox. The combination results at times in curious contrasts. In their first sojourn at court, the Fox and the Ape are among lords and ladies, suitors, a world of men, from the midst of which emerges the figure of the 'brave courtier:' in their second sojourn there, this world is suddenly transformed; for lords and ladies, suitors, men, we have the animals of Caxton's book, the Wolf, the Sheep, the Ass, and their like; it is the court of King Lion. Yet so spontaneous and creative are the acts of the poet's imagination that at no point in the long range of this satire are we checked by the sense of incongruity. The strange succession of scenes and figures, all admirably alive, the variety of artistic effects ranging from grotesqueness to romantic beauty, the sudden eruptions of strong personal feeling from levels of cool satire, the fluctuations of the style from crudity to masterliness, produce, in a small way, the sense of a world almost as real as that of the Faery Queen. This is mediæval satire at its best. The Italians, with whom Spenser was at this time rapidly becoming familiar, had already, for at least two generations, been cultivating the classic Roman form, and their lead had been followed by the head of the new English school, Sir Thomas W yatt: one might expect that Spenser, who from boyhood had been steeped in the classics, should also adopt this revived form. Nothing shows better the independence of his artistic eclecticism, his gift for taking here, there, and everywhere whatever appeals to his imagination, than the mediævalism of this his one satire.]

PROSOPOPOIA or MOTHER HUBBERDS TALE

It was the month in which the righteous Maide,
That, for disdaine of sinfull worlds upbraide,
Fled back to heaven, whence she was first conceived,
Into her silver bowre the Sunne received;
And the hot Syrian Dog on him awayting,
After the chafed Lyons cruell bayting,
Corrupted had th' ayre with his noysome breath,
And powr'd on th' earth plague, pestilence, and death.
Emongst the rest a wicked maladie
Raign'd emongst men, that manie did to die,
Depriv'd of sense and ordinarie reason;
That it to leaches seemed strange and geason.
My fortune was, mongst manie others moe,
To be partaker of their common woe;

And my weake bodie, set on fire with griefe,
Was rob'd of rest and naturall reliefe.
In this ill plight, there came to visite mee
Some friends, who, sorie my sad case to see,
Began to comfort me in chearfull wise,
And meanes of gladsome solace to devise.
But seeing kindly sleep refuse to doe
His office, and my feeble eyes forgoe,
They sought my troubled sense how to deceave
With talke, that might unquiet fancies reave;
And sitting all in seates about me round,
With pleasant tales (fit for that idle stound)
They cast in course to waste the wearie howres:
Some tolde of ladies, and their paramoures;
Some of brave knights, and their renowned squires;
Some of the faeries and their strange attires;
And some of giaunts hard to be beleeved;
That the delight thereof me much releeved.
Amongst the rest a good old woman was,
Hight Mother Hubberd, who did farre surpas
The rest in honest mirth, that seem'd her well:
She, when her turne was come her tale to tell,
Tolde of a strange adventure, that betided
Betwixt the Foxe and th' Ape by him misguided;
The which, for that my sense it greatly pleased,
All were my spirite heavie and diseased,
Ile write in termes, as she the same did say,
So well as I her words remember may.
No Muses aide me needes heretoo to call;
Base is the style, and matter meane withall.
Whilome (said she) before the world was civill,
The Foxe and th' Ape, disliking of their evill
And hard estate, determined to seeke
Their fortunes farre abroad, lyeke with his lyeke:
For both were craftie and unhappie witted:
Two fellowes might no where be better fitted.
The Foxe, that first this cause of griefe did finde,
Gan first thus plaine his case with words unkinde:
'Neighbour Ape, and my goship eke beside,
(Both two sure bands in friendship to be tide,)
To whom may I more trustely complaine
The evill plight that doth me sore constraine,
And hope thereof to finde due remedie?
Heare then my paine and inward agonie.
Thus manie yeares I now have spent and worne,
In meane regard, and basest fortunes scorne,
Dooing my countrey service as I might,
No lesse I dare saie than the prowdest wight;
And still I hoped to be up advaunced,
For my good parts; but still it hath mischaunced.
Now therefore that no lenger hope I see,

But froward fortune still to follow mee,
And losels lifted up on high, where I did looke,
I meane to turne the next leafe of the booke.
Yet ere that anie way I doo betake,
I meane my gossip privie first to make.
'Ah, my deare gossip!' answer'd then the Ape,
'Deeply doo your sad words my wits awhape,
Both for because your griefe doth great appeare,
And eke because my selfe am touched neare:
For I likewise have wasted much good time,
Still wayting to preferment up to clime,
Whilest others alwayes have before me stept,
And from my beard the fat away have swept;
That now unto despaire I gin to growe,
And meane for better winde about to throwe.
Therefore to me, my trustie friend, aread
Thy councell: two is better than one head.'
'Certes,' said he, 'I meane me to disguize
In some straunge habit, after uncouth wize,
Or like a pilgrime, or a lymiter,
Or like a gipsen, or a juggeler,
And so to wander to the worldes ende,
To seeke my fortune, where I may it mend:
For worse than that I have I cannot meete.
Wide is the world, I wote, and everie streete
Is full of fortunes and adventures straunge,
Continuallie subject unto chaunge.
Say, my faire brother, now, if this device
Doth like you, or may you to like entice.'
'Surely,' said th' Ape, 'it likes me wondrous well;
And would ye not poore fellowship expell,
My selfe would offer you t' accompanie
In this adventures chauncefull jeopardie.
For to wexe olde at home in idlenesse
Is disadventrous, and quite fortunelesse:
Abroad, where change is, good may gotten bee.'
The Foxe was glad, and quickly did agree:
So both resolv'd, the morrow next ensuing,
So soone as day appeard to peoples vewing,
On their intended journey to proceede;
And over night, whatso theretoo did neede
Each did prepare, in readines to bee.
The morrow next, so soone as one might see
Light out of heavens windowes forth to looke,
Both their habiliments unto them tooke,
And put themselves (a Gods name) on their way.
Whenas the Ape, beginning well to wey
This hard adventure, thus began t' advise:
'Now read, Sir Reynold, as ye be right wise,
What course ye weene is best for us to take,
That for our selves we may a living make.

Whether shall we professe some trade or skill?
Or shall we varie our device at will,
Even as new occasion appeares?
Or shall we tie our selves for certaine yeares
To anie service, or to anie place?
For it behoves, ere that into the race
We enter, to resolve first hereupon.'
'Now surely, brother,' said the Foxe anon,
'Ye have this matter motioned in season:
For everie thing that is begun with reason
Will come by readie meanes unto his end;
But things miscounselled must needs miswend.
Thus therefore I advize upon the case:
That not to anie certaine trade or place,
Nor anie man, we should our selves applie;
For why should he that is at libertie
Make himselfe bond? Sith then we are free borne,
Let us all servile base subjection scorne;
And as we bee sonnes of the world so wide,
Let us our fathers heritage divide,
And chalenge to our selves our portions dew
Of all the patrimonie, which a few
Now hold in hugger mugger in their hand,
And all the rest doo rob of good and land.
For now a few have all, and all have nought,
Yet all be brethren ylike dearly bought.
There is no right in this partition,
Ne was it so by institution
Ordained first, ne by the law of Nature,
But that she gave like blessing to each creture,
As well of worldly livelode as of life,
That there might be no difference nor strife,
Nor ought cald mine or thine: thrice happie then
Was the condition of mortall men.
That was the golden age of Saturne old,
But this might better be the world of gold:
For without golde now nothing wilbe got.
Therefore (if please you) this shalbe our plot:
We will not be of anie occupation;
Let such vile vassalls, borne to base vocation,
Drudge in the world, and for their living droyle,
Which have no wit to live withouten toyle.
But we will walke about the world at pleasure,
Like two free men, and make our ease a treasure.
Free men some beggers call; but they be free,
And they which call them so more beggers bee:
For they doo swinke and sweate to feed the other,
Who live like lords of that which they doo gather,
And yet doo never thanke them for the same,
But as their due by nature doo it clame.
Such will we fashion both our selves to bee,

Lords of the world, and so will wander free
Where so us listeth, uncontrol'd of anie.
Hard is our hap, if we (emongst so manie)
Light not on some that may our state amend;
Sildome but some good commeth ere the end.'
Well seemd the Ape to like this ordinaunce:
Yet, well considering of the circumstaunce,
As pausing in great doubt, awhile he staid,
And afterwards with grave advizement said:
'I cannot, my lief brother, like but well
The purpose of the complot which ye tell:
For well I wot (compar'd to all the rest
Of each degree) that beggers life is best:
And they that thinke themselves the best of all
Oft-times to begging are content to fall.
But this I wot withall, that we shall ronne
Into great daunger, like to bee undonne,
Thus wildly to wander in the worlds eye,
Without pasport or good warrantie,
For feare least we like rogues should be reputed,
And for eare marked beasts abroad be bruted.
Therefore I read that we our counsells call,
How to prevent this mischiefe ere it fall,
And how we may, with most securitie,
Beg amongst those that beggers doo defie.'
'Right well, deere gossip, ye advized have,'
Said then the Foxe, 'but I this doubt will save:
For ere we farther passe, I will devise
A pasport for us both in fittest wize,
And by the names of souldiers us protect;
That now is thought a civile begging sect.
Be you the souldier, for you likest are
For manly semblance, and small skill in warre:
I will but wayte on you, and, as occasion
Falls out, my selfe fit for the same will fashion.'
The pasport ended, both they forward went;
The Ape clad souldierlike, fit for th' intent,
In a blew jacket with a crosse of redd
And manie slits, as if that he had shedd
Much blood throgh many wounds therein receaved,
Which had the use of his right arme bereaved.
Upon his head an old Scotch cap he wore,
With a plume feather all to peeces tore:
His breeches were made after the new cut,
Al Portugese, loose like an emptie gut;
And his hose broken high above the heeling,
And his shooes beaten out with traveling.
But neither sword nor dagger he did beare;
Seemes that no foes revengement he did feare;
In stead of them a handsome bat he held,
On which he leaned, as one farre in elde.

Shame light on him, that through so false illusion
Doth turne the name of souldiers to abusion,
And that, which is the noblest mysterie,
Brings to reproach and common infamie.
Long they thus travailed, yet never met
Adventure, which might them a working set:
Yet manie waies they sought, and manie tryed;
Yet for their purposes none fit espyed.
At last they chaunst to meete upon the way
A simple Husbandman in garments gray;
Yet, though his vesture were but meane and bace,
A good yeoman he was of honest place,
And more for thrift did care than for gay clothing:
Gay without good is good hearts greatest loathing.
The Foxe, him spying, bad the Ape him dight
To play his part, for loe! he was in sight
That (if he er'd not) should them entertaine,
And yeeld them timely profite for their paine.
Eftsoones the Ape himselfe gan up to reare,
And on his shoulders high his bat to beare,
As if good service he were fit to doo;
But little thrift for him he did it too:
And stoutly forward he his steps did straine,
That like a handsome swaine it him became.
When as they nigh approached, that good man,
Seeing them wander loosly, first began
T' enquire, of custome, what and whence they were.
To whom the Ape: 'I am a souldiere,
That late in warres have spent my deerest blood,
And in long service lost both limbs and good;
And now, constrain'd that trade to overgive,
I driven am to seeke some meanes to live:
Which might it you in pitie please t' afford,
I would be readie, both in deed and word,
To doo you faithfull service all my dayes.
This yron world' (that same he weeping sayes)
'Brings downe the stowtest hearts to lowest state:
For miserie doth bravest mindes abate,
And make them seeke for that they wont to scorne,
Of fortune and of hope at once forlorne.'
The honest man, that heard him thus complaine,
Was griev'd, as he had felt part of his paine;
And, well disposd' him some reliefe to showe,
Askt if in husbandrie he ought did knowe,
To plough, to plant, to reap, to rake, to sowe,
To hedge, to ditch, to thrash, to thetch, to mowe;
Or to what labour els he was prepar'd:
For husbands life is labourous and hard.
Whenas the Ape him hard so much to talke
Of labour, that did from his liking balke,
He would have slipt the coller handsomly,

And to him said: 'Good sir, full glad am I
To take what paines may anie living wight:
But my late maymed limbs lack wonted might
To doo their kindly services, as needeth:
Scarce this right hand the mouth with diet feedeth;
So that it may no painfull worke endure,
Ne to strong labour can it selfe enure.
But if that anie other place you have,
Which askes small paines, but thriftines to save,
Or care to overlooke, or trust to gather,
Ye may me trust as your owne ghostly father.'
With that the Husbandman gan him avize,
That it for him were fittest exercise
Cattell to keep, or grounds to oversee;
And asked him, if he could willing bee
To keep his sheep, or to attend his swyne,
Or watch his mares, or take his charge of kyne.
'Gladly,' said he, 'what ever such like paine
Ye put on me, I will the same sustaine:
But gladliest I of your fleecie sheepe
(Might it you please) would take on me the keep.
For ere that unto armes I me betooke,
Unto my fathers sheepe I usde to looke,
That yet the skill thereof I have not loste:
Thereto right well this curdog by my coste'
(Meaning the Foxe) 'will serve, my sheepe to gather,
And drive to follow after their belwether.'
The Husbandman was meanly well content,
Triall to make of his endevourment,
And home him leading, lent to him the charge
Of all his flocke, with libertie full large,
Giving accompt of th' annuall increce
Both of their lambes, and of their woolley fleece.
Thus is this Ape become a shepheard swaine,
And the false Foxe his dog: (God give them paine)
For ere the yeare have halfe his course out-run,
And doo returne from whence he first begun,
They shall him make an ill accompt of thrift.
Now whenas Time, flying with winges swift,
Expired had the terme, that these two javels
Should render up a reckning of their travels
Unto their master, which it of them sought,
Exceedingly they troubled were in thought,
Ne wist what answere unto him to frame,
Ne how to scape great punishment, or shame,
For their false treason and vile theeverie.
For not a lambe of all their flockes supply
Had they to shew; but ever as they bred,
They slue them, and upon their fleshes fed:
For that disguised dog lov'd blood to spill,
And drew the wicked shepheard to his will.

So twixt them both they not a lambkin left,
And when lambes fail'd, the old sheepes lives they reft;
That how t' acquite themselves unto their lord
They were in doubt, and flatly set abord.
The Foxe then counsel'd th' Ape for to require
Respite till morrow t' answere his desire:
For times delay new hope of helpe still breeds.
The goodman granted, doubting nought their deeds,
And bad, next day that all should readie be.
But they more subtill meaning had than he:
For the next morrowes meed they closely ment,
For feare of afterclaps, for to prevent:
And that same evening, when all shrowded were
In careles sleep, they, without care or feare,
Cruelly fell upon their flock in folde,
And of them slew at pleasure what they wolde:
Of which whenas they feasted had their fill,
For a full complement of all their ill,
They stole away, and tooke their hastie flight,
Carried in clowdes of all-concealing night.
So was the Husbandman left to his losse,
And they unto their fortunes change to tosse.
After which sort they wandered long while,
Abusing manie through their cloaked guile;
That at the last they gan to be descryed
Of everie one, and all their sleights espyed:
So as their begging now them failed quyte;
For none would give, but all men would them wyte.
Yet would they take no paines to get their living,
But seeke some other way to gaine by giving,
Much like to begging, but much better named;
For manie beg, which are thereof ashamed.
And now the Foxe had gotten him a gowne,
And th' Ape a cassocke sidelong hanging downe;
For they their occupation meant to change,
And now in other state abroad to range:
For since their souldiers pas no better spedd,
They forg'd another, as for clerkes booke-redd.
Who passing foorth, as their adventures fell,
Through manie haps, which needs not here to tell,
At length chaunst with a formall Priest to meete,
Whom they in civill manner first did greete,
And after askt an almes for Gods deare love.
The man straight way his choler up did move,
And with reproachfull tearmes gan them revile,
For following that trade so base and vile;
And askt what license or what pas they had.
'Ah!' said the Ape, as sighing wondrous sad,
'Its an hard case, when men of good deserving
Must either driven be perforce to sterving,
Or asked for their pas by everie squib,

That list at will them to revile or snib:
And yet (God wote) small oddes I often see
Twixt them that aske, and them that asked bee.
Natheles because you shall not us misdeeme,
But that we are as honest as we seeme,
Yee shall our pasport at your pleasure see,
And then ye will (I hope) well mooved bee.'
Which when the Priest beheld, he vew'd it nere,
As if therein some text he studying were,
But little els (God wote) could thereof skill:
For read he could not evidence nor will,
Ne tell a written word, ne write a letter,
Ne make one title worse, ne make one better.
Of such deep learning little had he neede,
Ne yet of Latine, ne of Greeke, that breede
Doubts mongst divines, and difference of texts,
From whence arise diversitie of sects,
And hatefull heresies, of God abhor'd.
But this good Sir did follow the plaine word,
Ne medled with their controversies vaine:
All his care was, his service well to saine,
And to read homelies upon holidayes;
When that was done, he might attend his playes:
An easie life, and fit High God to please.
He, having overlookt their pas at ease,
Gan at the length them to rebuke againe,
That no good trade of life did entertaine,
But lost their time in wandring loose abroad;
Seeing the world, in which they bootles boad,
Had wayes enough for all therein to live;
Such grace did God unto his creatures give.
Said then the Foxe: 'Who hath the world not tride
From the right way full eath may wander wide.
We are but novices, new come abroad,
We have not yet the tract of anie troad,
Nor on us taken anie state of life,
But readie are of anie to make preife.
Therefore might please you, which the world have proved,
Us to advise, which forth but lately moved,
Of some good course, that we might undertake,
Ye shall for ever us your bondmen make.'
The Priest gan wexe halfe proud to be so praide,
And thereby willing to affoord them aide;
'It seemes,' said he, 'right well that ye be clerks,
Both by your wittie words and by your werks.
Is not that name enough to make a living
To him that hath a whit of Natures giving?
How manie honest men see ye arize
Daylie thereby, and grow to goodly prize?
To deanes, to archdeacons, to commissaries,
To lords, to principalls, to prebendaries;

All jolly prelates, worthie rule to beare,
Who ever them envie: yet spite bites neare.
Why should ye doubt, then, but that ye like-wise
Might unto some of those in time arise?
In the meane time to live in good estate,
Loving that love, and hating those that hate;
Being some honest curate, or some vicker,
Content with little in condition sicker.'
'Ah! but,' said th' Ape, 'the charge is wondrous great,
To feed mens soules, and hath an heavie threat.'
'To feede mens soules,' quoth he, 'is not in man:
For they must feed themselves, doo what we can.
We are but charg'd to lay the meate before:
Eate they that list, we need to doo no more.
But God it is that feedes them with his grace,
The bread of life powr'd downe from heavenly place.
Therefore said he, that with the budding rod
Did rule the Jewes, All shalbe taught of God.
That same hath Jesus Christ now to him raught,
By whom the flock is rightly fed and taught:
He is the shepheard, and the priest is hee;
We but his shepheard swaines ordain'd to bee.
Therefore herewith doo not your selfe dismay;
Ne is the paines so great, but beare ye may;
For not so great, as it was wont of yore,
It 's now a dayes, ne halfe so streight and sore.
They whilome used duly everie day
Their service and their holie things to say,
At morne and even, besides their anthemes sweete,
Their penie masses, and their complynes meete,
Their dirges, their trentals, and their shrifts,
Their memories, their singings, and their gifts.
Now all those needlesse works are laid away;
Now once a weeke, upon the Sabbath day,
It is enough to doo our small devotion,
And then to follow any merrie motion.
Ne are we tyde to fast, but when we list,
Ne to weare garments base of wollen twist,
But with the finest silkes us to aray,
That before God we may appeare more gay,
Resembling Aarons glorie in his place:
For farre unfit it is, that person bace
Should with vile cloaths approach Gods majestie,
Whom no uncleannes may approachen nie:
Or that all men, which anie master serve,
Good garments for their service should deserve,
But he that serves the Lord of Hoasts Most High,
And that in highest place, t' approach him nigh,
And all the peoples prayers to present
Before his throne, as on ambassage sent
Both too and fro, should not deserve to weare

A garment better than of wooll or heare.
Beside, we may have lying by our sides
Our lovely lasses, or bright shining brides:
We be not tyde to wilfull chastitie,
But have the gospell of free libertie.'
By that he ended had his ghostly sermon,
The Foxe was well induc'd to be a parson;
And of the Priest eftsoones gan to enquire,
How to a benefice he might aspire.
'Marie, there,' said the Priest, 'is arte indeed:
Much good deep learning one thereout may reed;
For that the ground-worke is, and end of all,
How to obtaine a beneficiall.
First therefore, when ye have in handsome wise
Your selfe attyred, as you can devise,
Then to some noble man your selfe applye,
Or other great one in the worldes eye,
That hath a zealous disposition
To God, and so to his religion.
There must thou fashion eke a godly zeale,
Such as no carpers may contrayre reveale:
For each thing fained ought more warie bee.
There thou must walke in sober gravitee,
And seeme as saintlike as Saint Radegund:
Fast much, pray oft, looke lowly on the ground,
And unto everie one doo curtesie meeke:
These lookes (nought saying) doo a benefice seeke,
And be thou sure one not to lacke or long.
But if thee list unto the court to throng,
And there to hunt after the hoped pray,
Then must thou thee dispose another way:
For there thou needs must learne to laugh, to lie,
To face, to forge, to scoffe, to companie,
To crouche, to please, to be a beetle stock
Of thy great masters will, to scorne, or mock:
So maist thou chaunce mock out a benefice,
Unlesse thou canst one conjure by device,
Or cast a figure for a bishoprick:
And if one could, it were but a schoole trick.
These be the wayes, by which without reward
Livings in court be gotten, though full hard.
For nothing there is done without a fee:
The courtier needes must recompenced bee
With a benevolence, or have in gage
The primitias of your parsonage:
Scarse can a bishoprick forpas them by,
But that it must be gelt in privitie.
Doo not thou therefore seeke a living there,
But of more private persons seeke elswhere,
Whereas thou maist compound a better penie,
Ne let thy learning question'd be of anie.

For some good gentleman, that hath the right
Unto his church for to present a wight,
Will cope with thee in reasonable wise;
That if the living yerely doo arise
To fortie pound, that then his yongest sonne
Shall twentie have, and twentie thou hast wonne:
Thou hast it wonne, for it is of franke gift,
And he will care for all the rest to shift;
Both that the bishop may admit of thee,
And that therein thou maist maintained bee.
This is the way for one that is unlern'd
Living to get, and not to be discern'd.
But they that are great clerkes have nearer wayes,
For learning sake to living them to raise:
Yet manie eke of them (God wote) are driven,
T' accept a benefice in peeces riven.
How saist thou (friend) have I not well discourst
Upon this common place (though plaine, not wourst)?
Better a short tale than a bad long shriving.
Needes anie more to learne to get a living?'
'Now sure, and by my hallidome,' quoth he,
'Ye a great master are in your degree:
Great thankes I yeeld you for your discipline,
And doo not doubt, but duly to encline
My wits theretoo, as ye shall shortly heare.'
The Priest him wisht good speed, and well to fare.
So parted they, as eithers way them led.
But th' Ape and Foxe ere long so well them sped,
Through the Priests holesome counsell lately tought,
And throgh their own faire handling wisely wroght,
That they a benefice twixt them obtained;
And craftie Reynold was a priest ordained,
And th' Ape his parish clarke procur'd to bee.
Then made they revell route and goodly glee.
But ere long time had passed, they so ill
Did order their affaires, that th' evill will
Of all their parishners they had constrain'd;
Who to the ordinarie of them complain'd,
How fowlie they their offices abusd',
And them of crimes and heresies accusd';
That pursivants he often for them sent:
But they neglected his commaundement.
So long persisted obstinate and bolde,
Till at the length he published to holde
A visitation, and them cyted thether:
Then was high time their wits about to geather.
What did they then, but made a composition
With their next neighbor priest, for light condition,
To whom their living they resigned quight
For a few pence, and ran away by night.
So passing through the countrey in disguize,

They fled farre off, where none might them surprize,
And after that long straied here and there,
Through everie field and forrest farre and nere;
Yet never found occasion for their tourne,
But, almost sterv'd, did much lament and mourne.
At last they chaunst to meete upon the way
The Mule, all deckt in goodly rich aray,
With bells and bosses, that full lowdly rung,
And costly trappings, that to ground downe hung.
Lowly they him saluted in meeke wise;
But he through pride and fatnes gan despise
Their meanesse; scarce vouchsafte them to requite.
Whereat the Foxe deep groning in his sprite,
Said: 'Ah, Sir Mule! now blessed be the day,
That I see you so goodly and so gay
In your attyres, and eke your silken hyde
Fil'd with round flesh, that everie bone doth hide.
Seemes that in fruitfull pastures ye doo live,
Or Fortune doth you secret favour give.'
'Foolish Foxe!' said the Mule, 'thy wretched need
Praiseth the thing that doth thy sorrow breed.
For well I weene, thou canst not but envie
My wealth, compar'd to thine owne miserie,
That art so leane and meagre waxen late,
That scarse thy legs uphold thy feeble gate.'
'Ay me!' said then the Foxe, 'whom evill hap
Unworthy in such wretchednes doth wrap,
And makes the scorne of other beasts to bee.
But read (faire sir, of grace) from whence come yee?
Or what of tidings you abroad doo heare?
Newes may perhaps some good unweeting beare.'
'From royall court I lately came,' said he,
'Where all the braverie that eye may see,
And all the happinesse that heart desire,
Is to be found; he nothing can admire,
That hath not seene that heavens portracture:
But tidings there is none, I you assure,
Save that which common is, and knowne to all,
That courtiers as the tide doo rise and fall.'
'But tell us,' said the Ape, 'we doo you pray,
Who now in court doth beare the greatest sway:
That, if such fortune doo to us befall,
We may seeke favour of the best of all.'
'Marie,' said he, 'the highest now in grace,
Be the wilde beasts, that swiftest are in chase;
For in their speedie course and nimble flight
The Lyon now doth take the most delight:
But chieflie joyes on foote them to beholde,
Enchaste with chaine and circulet of golde.
So wilde a beast so tame ytaught to bee,
And buxome to his bands, is joy to see;

So well his golden circlet him beseemeth:
But his late chayne his Liege unmeete esteemeth;
For so brave beasts she loveth best to see
In the wilde forrest raunging fresh and free.
Therefore if fortune thee in court to live,
In case thou ever there wilt hope to thrive,
To some of these thou must thy selfe apply:
Els as a thistle-downe in th' ayre doth flie,
So vainly shalt thou too and fro be tost,
And loose thy labour and thy fruitles cost.
And yet full few which follow them, I see,
For vertues bare regard advaunced bee,
But either for some gainfull benefit,
Or that they may for their owne turnes be fit.
Nath'les, perhaps ye things may handle soe,
That ye may better thrive than thousands moe.'
'But,' said the Ape, 'how shall we first come in,
That after we may favour seeke to win?'
'How els,' said he, 'but with a good bold face,
And with big words, and with a stately pace,
That men may thinke of you, in generall,
That to be in you, which is not at all:
For not by that which is, the world now deemeth,
(As it was wont) but by that same that seemeth.
Ne do I doubt, but that ye well can fashion
Your selves theretoo, according to occasion:
So fare ye well; good courtiers may ye bee.'
So, proudlie neighing, from them parted hee.
Then gan this craftie couple to devize,
How for the court themselves they might aguize:
For thither they themselves meant to addresse,
In hope to finde there happier successe.
So well they shifted, that the Ape anon
Himselfe had cloathed like a gentleman,
And the slie Foxe, as like to be his groome;
That to the court in seemly sort they come.
Where the fond Ape, himselfe uprearing hy
Upon his tiptoes, stalketh stately by,
As if he were some great magnifico,
And boldlie doth amongst the boldest go;
And his man Reynold, with fine counterfesaunce,
Supports his credite and his countenaunce.
Then gan the courtiers gaze on everie side,
And stare on him, with big lookes basen wide,
Wondring what mister wight he was, and whence:
For he was clad in strange accoustrements,
Fashion'd with queint devises never seene
In court before, yet there all fashions beene:
Yet he them in newfanglenesse did pas.
But his behaviour altogether was
Alla Turchesca, much the more admyr'd,

And his lookes loftie, as if he aspyr'd
To dignitie, and sdeign'd the low degree;
That all which did such strangenesse in him see
By secrete meanes gan of his state enquire,
And privily his servant thereto hire:
Who, throughly arm'd against such coverture,
Reported unto all, that he was sure
A noble gentleman of high regard,
Which through the world had with long travel far'd,
And seene the manners of all beasts on ground;
Now here arriv'd, to see if like he found.
Thus did the Ape at first him credit gaine,
Which afterwards he wisely did maintaine
With gallant showe, and daylie more augment
Through his fine feates and courtly complement;
For he could play, and daunce, and vaute, and spring,
And all that els pertaines to reveling,
Onely through kindly aptnes of his joynts.
Besides he could doo manie other poynts,
The which in court him served to good stead:
For he mongst ladies could their fortunes read
Out of their hands, and merie leasings tell,
And juggle finely, that became him well:
But he so light was at legier demaine,
That what he toucht came not to light againe;
Yet would he laugh it out, and proudly looke,
And tell them that they greatly him mistooke.
So would he scoffe them out with mockerie,
For he therein had great felicitie;
And with sharp quips joy'd others to deface,
Thinking that their disgracing did him grace:
So whilst that other like vaine wits he pleased
And made to laugh, his heart was greatly eased.
But the right gentle minde would bite his lip,
To heare the javell so good men to nip:
For though the vulgar yeeld an open eare,
And common courtiers love to gybe and fleare
At everie thing, which they heare spoken ill,
And the best speaches with ill meaning spill;
Yet the brave courtier, in whose beauteous thought
Regard of honour harbours more than ought,
Doth loath such base condition, to backbite
Anies good name for envie or despite.
He stands on tearmes of honourable minde,
Ne will be carried with the common winde
Of courts inconstant mutabilitie,
Ne after everie tattling fable flie;
But heares and sees the follies of the rest,
And thereof gathers for himselfe the best.
He will not creepe, nor crouche with fained face,
But walkes upright with comely stedfast pace,

And unto all doth yeeld due curtesie;
But not with kissed hand belowe the knee,
As that same apish crue is wont to doo:
For he disdaines himselfe t' embase there-too.
He hates fowle leasings, and vile flatterie,
Two filthie blots in noble gentrie;
And lothefull idlenes he doth detest,
The canker worme of everie gentle brest;
The which to banish with faire exercise
Of knightly feates, he daylie doth devise:
Now menaging the mouthes of stubborne steedes,
Now practising the proofe of warlike deedes,
Now his bright armes assaying, now his speare,
Now the nigh aymed ring away to beare:
At other times he casts to sew the chace
Of swift wilde beasts, or runne on foote a race,
T' enlarge his breath (large breath in armes most needfull)
Or els by wrestling to wex strong and heedfull,
Or his stiffe armes to stretch with eughen bowe,
And manly legs, still passing too and fro,
Without a gowned beast him fast beside;
A vaine ensample of the Persian pride,
Who after he had wonne th' Assyrian foe,
Did ever after scorne on foote to goe.
Thus when this courtly gentleman with toyle
Himselfe hath wearied, he doth recoyle
Unto his rest, and there with sweete delight
Of musicks skill revives his toyled spright;
Or els with loves and ladies gentle sports,
The joy of youth, himselfe he recomforts:
Or lastly, when the bodie list to pause,
His minde unto the Muses he withdrawes;
Sweete Ladie Muses, ladies of delight,
Delights of life, and ornaments of light:
With whom he close confers, with wise discourse,
Of Natures workes, of heavens continuall course,
Of forreine lands, of people different,
Of kingdomes change, of divers government,
Of dreadfull battailes of renowmed knights;
With which he kindleth his ambitious sprights
To like desire and praise of noble fame,
The onely upshot whereto he doth ayme.
For all his minde on honour fixed is,
To which he levels all his purposis,
And in his princes service spends his dayes,
Not so much for to gaine, or for to raise
Himselfe to high degree, as for his grace,
And in his liking to winne worthie place,
Through due deserts and comely carriage,
In whatso please employ his personage,
That may be matter meete to gaine him praise;

For he is fit to use in all assayes,
Whether for armes and warlike amenaunce,
Or else for wise and civill governaunce.
For he is practiz'd well in policie,
And thereto doth his courting most applie:
To learne the enterdeale of princes strange,
To marke th' intent of counsells, and the change
Of states, and eke of private men somewhile,
Supplanted by fine falshood and faire guile;
Of all the which he gathereth what is fit
T' enrich the storehouse of his powerfull wit,
Which through wise speaches and grave conference
He daylie eekes, and brings to excellence.
Such is the rightfull courtier in his kinde:
But unto such the Ape lent not his minde;
Such were for him no fit companions,
Such would descrie his lewd conditions:
But the yong lustie gallants he did chose
To follow, meete to whom he might disclose
His witlesse pleasance and ill pleasing vaine.
A thousand wayes he them could entertaine,
With all the thriftles games that may be found;
With mumming and with masking all around,
With dice, with cards, with balliards farre unfit,
With shuttelcocks, misseeming manlie wit,
With courtizans, and costly riotize,
Whereof still somewhat to his share did rize:
Ne, them to pleasure, would he sometimes scorne
A pandares coate (so basely was he borne);
Thereto he could fine loving verses frame,
And play the poet oft. But ah! for shame,
Let not sweete poets praise, whose onely pride
Is vertue to advaunce, and vice deride,
Be with the worke of losels wit defamed,
Ne let such verses poetrie be named.
Yet he the name on him would rashly take,
Maugre the sacred Muses, and it make
A servant to the vile affection
Of such as he depended most upon,
And with the sugrie sweete thereof allure
Chast ladies eares to fantasies impure.
To such delights the noble wits he led
Which him reliev'd, and their vaine humours fed
With fruitles follies and unsound delights.
But if perhaps into their noble sprights
Desire of honor or brave thought of armes
Did ever creepe, then with his wicked charmes
And strong conceipts he would it drive away,
Ne suffer it to house there halfe a day.
And whenso love of letters did inspire
Their gentle wits, and kindly wise desire,

That chieflie doth each noble minde adorne,
Then he would scoffe at learning, and eke scorne
The sectaries thereof, as people base
And simple men, which never came in place
Of worlds affaires, but, in darke corners mewd,
Muttred of matters, as their bookes them shewd,
Ne other knowledge ever did attaine,
But with their gownes their gravitie maintaine.
From them he would his impudent lewde speach
Against Gods holie ministers oft reach,
And mocke divines and their profession:
What else then did he by progression,
But mocke High God himselfe, whom they professe?
But what car'd he for God, or godlinesse?
All his care was himselfe how to advaunce,
And to uphold his courtly countenaunce
By all the cunning meanes he could devise;
Were it by honest wayes, or otherwise,
He made small choyce: yet sure his honestie
Got him small gaines, but shameles flatterie,
And filthie brocage, and unseemly shifts,
And borowe base, and some good ladies gifts:
But the best helpe, which chiefly him sustain'd,
Was his man Raynolds purchase which he gain'd.
For he was school'd by kinde in all the skill
Of close conveyance, and each practise ill
Of coosinage and cleanly knaverie,
Which oft maintain'd his masters braverie.
Besides, he usde another slipprie slight,
In taking on himselfe, in common sight,
False personages fit for everie sted,
With which he thousands cleanly coosined:
Now like a merchant, merchants to deceave,
With whom his credite he did often leave
In gage, for his gay masters hopelesse dett:
Now like a lawyer, when he land would lett,
Or sell fee-simples in his masters name,
Which he had never, nor ought like the same:
Then would he be a broker, and draw in
Both wares and money, by exchange to win:
Then would he seeme a farmer, that would sell
Bargaines of woods, which he did lately fell,
Or corne, or cattle, or such other ware,
Thereby to coosin men not well aware;
Of all the which there came a secret fee
To th' Ape, that he his countenaunce might bee.
Besides all this, he usd' oft to beguile
Poore suters, that in court did haunt some while:
For he would learne their busines secretly,
And then informe his master hastely,
That he by meanes might cast them to prevent,

And beg the sute the which the other ment.
Or otherwise false Reynold would abuse
The simple suter, and wish him to chuse
His master, being one of great regard
In court, to compas anie sute not hard,
In case his paines were recompenst with reason:
So would he worke the silly man by treason
To buy his masters frivolous good will,
That had not power to doo him good or ill.
So pitifull a thing is suters state.
Most miserable man, whom wicked fate
Hath brought to court, to sue for had ywist,
That few have found, and manie one hath mist!
Full little knowest thou that hast not tride,
What hell it is, in suing long to bide:
To loose good dayes, that might be better spent;
To wast long nights in pensive discontent;
To speed to day, to be put back to morrow;
To feed on hope, to pine with feare and sorrow;
To have thy Princes grace, yet want her Peeres;
To have thy asking, yet waite manie yeeres;
To fret thy soule with crosses and with cares;
To eate thy heart through comfortlesse dispaires;
To fawne, to crowche, to waite, to ride, to ronne,
To spend, to give, to want, to be undonne.
Unhappie wight, borne to desastrous end,
That doth his life in so long tendance spend!
Who ever leaves sweete home, where meane estate
In safe assurance, without strife or hate,
Findes all things needfull for contentment meeke,
And will to court, for shadowes vaine to seeke,
Or hope to gaine, himselfe will a daw trie:
That curse God send unto mine enemie!
For none but such as this bold Ape unblest
Can ever thrive in that unluckie quest;
Or such as hath a Reynold to his man,
That by his shifts his master furnish can.
But yet this Foxe could not so closely hide
His craftie feates, but that they were descride
At length, by such as sate in justice seate,
Who for the same him fowlie did entreate;
And having worthily him punished,
Out of the court for ever banished.
And now the Ape, wanting his huckster man,
That wont provide his necessaries, gan
To growe into great lacke, ne could upholde
His countenaunce in those his garments olde;
Ne new ones could he easily provide,
Though all men him uncased gan deride,
Like as a puppit placed in a play,
Whose part once past all men bid take away:

So that he driven was to great distresse,
And shortly brought to hopelesse wretchednesse.
Then, closely as he might, he cast to leave
The court, not asking any passe or leave;
But ran away in his rent rags by night,
Ne ever stayd in place, ne spake to wight,
Till that the Foxe, his copesmate, he had found;
To whome complayning his unhappy stound,
At last againe with him in travell joynd,
And with him far'd some better chaunce to fynde.
So in the world long time they wandered,
And mickle want and hardnesse suffered;
That them repented much so foolishly
To come so farre to seeke for misery,
And leave the sweetnes of contented home,
Though eating hipps and drinking watry fome.
Thus as they them complayned too and fro,
Whilst through the forest rechlesse they did goe,
Lo! where they spide, how in a gloomy glade
The Lyon sleeping lay in secret shade,
His crowne and scepter lying him beside,
And having doft for heate his dreadfull hide:
Which when they sawe, the Ape was sore afrayde,
And would have fled with terror all dismayde.
But him the Foxe with hardy words did stay,
And bad him put all cowardize away:
For now was time (if ever they would hope)
To ayme their counsels to the fairest scope,
And them for ever highly to advaunce,
In case the good, which their owne happie chaunce
Them freely offred, they would wisely take.
Scarse could the Ape yet speake, so did he quake;
Yet, as he could, he askt how good might growe,
Where nought but dread and death do seeme in show.
'Now,' sayd he, 'whiles the Lyon sleepeth sound,
May we his crowne and mace take from the ground,
And eke his skinne, the terror of the wood,
Wherewith we may our selves (if we thinke good)
Make kings of beasts, and lords of forests all,
Subject unto that powre imperiall.'
'Ah! but,' sayd the Ape, 'who is so bold a wretch,
That dare his hardy hand to those out stretch,
When as he knowes his meede, if he be spide,
To be a thousand deathes, and shame beside?'
'Fond Ape!' sayd then the Foxe, 'into whose brest
Never crept thought of honor nor brave gest,
Who will not venture life a king to be,
And rather rule and raigne in soveraign see,
Than dwell in dust inglorious and bace,
Where none shall name the number of his place?
One joyous houre in blisfull happines,

I chose before a life of wretchednes.
Be therefore counselled herein by me,
And shake off this vile harted cowardree.
If he awake, yet is not death the next,
For we may coulor it with some pretext
Of this or that, that may excuse the cryme:
Else we may flye; thou to a tree mayst clyme,
And I creepe under ground; both from his reach:
Therefore be rul'd to doo as I doo teach.'
The Ape, that earst did nought but chill and quake,
Now gan some courage unto him to take,
And was content to attempt that enterprise,
Tickled with glorie and rash covetise.
But first gan question, whither should assay
Those royall ornaments to steale away.
'Marie, that shall your selfe,' quoth he theretoo,
'For ye be fine and nimble it to doo;
Of all the beasts which in the forrests bee
Is not a fitter for this turne than yee:
Therefore, mine owne deare brother, take good hart,
And ever thinke a kingdome is your part.'
Loath was the Ape, though praised, to adventer,
Yet faintly gan into his worke to enter,
Afraid of everie leafe that stir'd him by,
And everie stick that underneath did ly:
Upon his tiptoes nicely he up went,
For making noyse, and still his eare he lent
To everie sound that under heaven blew;
Now went, now stept, now crept, now backward drew,
That it good sport had been him to have eyde.
Yet at the last (so well he him applyde)
Through his fine handling and cleanly play
He all those royall signes had stolne away,
And with the Foxes helpe them borne aside
Into a secret corner unespide.
Whether whenas they came, they fell at words,
Whether of them should be the lord of lords:
For th' Ape was stryfull and ambicious,
And the Foxe guilefull and most covetous;
That neither pleased was, to have the rayne
Twixt them divided into even twaine,
But either algates would be lord alone:
For love and lordship bide no paragone.
'I am most worthie,' said the Ape, 'sith I
For it did put my life in jeopardie:
Thereto I am in person and in stature
Most like a man, the lord of everie creature;
So that it seemeth I was made to raigne,
And borne to be a kingly soveraigne.'
'Nay,' said the Foxe, 'Sir Ape, you are astray:
For though to steale the diademe away

Were the worke of your nimble hand, yet I
Did first devise the plot by pollicie;
So that it wholly springeth from my wit:
For which also I claime my selfe more fit
Than you to rule: for government of state
Will without wisedome soone be ruinate.
And where ye claime your selfe for outward shape
Most like a man, man is not like an ape
In his chiefe parts, that is, in wit and spirite;
But I therein most like to him doo merite,
For my slie wyles and subtill craftinesse,
The title of the kingdome to possesse.
Nath'les (my brother) since we passed are
Unto this point, we will appease our jarre;
And I with reason meete will rest content,
That ye shall have both crowne and government,
Upon condition that ye ruled bee
In all affaires, and counselled by mee;
And that ye let none other ever drawe
Your minde from me, but keepe this as a lawe:
And hereupon an oath unto me plight.'
The Ape was glad to end the strife so light,
And thereto swore: for who would not oft sweare,
And oft unsweare, a diademe to beare?
Then freely up those royall spoyles he tooke;
Yet at the Lyons skin he inly quooke;
But it dissembled; and upon his head
The crowne, and on his backe the skin, he did,
And the false Foxe him helped to array.
Then when he was all dight he tooke his way
Into the forest, that he might be seene
Of the wilde beasts in his new glory sheene.
There the two first whome he encountred were
The Sheepe and th' Asse, who, striken both with feare
At sight of him, gan fast away to flye;
But unto them the Foxe alowd did cry,
And in the kings name bad them both to stay,
Upon the payne that thereof follow may.
Hardly naythles were they restrayned so,
Till that the Foxe forth toward them did goe,
And there disswaded them from needlesse feare,
For that the king did favour to them beare;
And therefore dreadles bad them come to corte:
For no wild beasts should do them any torte
There or abroad, ne would his Majestye
Use them but well, with gracious clemencye,
As whome he knew to him both fast and true.
So he perswaded them, with homage due
Themselves to humble to the Ape prostrate,
Who, gently to them bowing in his gate,
Receyved them with chearefull entertayne.

Thenceforth proceeding with his princely trayne,
He shortly met the Tygre, and the Bore,
Which with the simple Camell raged sore
In bitter words, seeking to take occasion,
Upon his fleshly corpse to make invasion:
But soone as they this mock-king did espy,
Their troublous strife they stinted by and by,
Thinking indeed that it the Lyon was.
He then, to prove whether his powre would pas
As currant, sent the Foxe to them streight way,
Commaunding them their cause of strife bewray;
And, if that wrong on eyther side there were,
That he should warne the wronger to appeare
The morrow next at court, it to defend;
In the meane time upon the king t' attend.
The subtile Foxe so well his message sayd,
That the proud beasts him readily obayd:
Whereby the Ape in wondrous stomack woxe,
Strongly encorag'd by the crafty Foxe;
That king indeed himselfe he shortly thought,
And all the beasts him feared as they ought,
And followed unto his palaice hye;
Where taking conge, each one by and by
Departed to his home in dreadfull awe,
Full of the feared sight, which late they sawe.
The Ape, thus seized of the regall throne,
Eftsones by counsell of the Foxe alone
Gan to provide for all things in assurance,
That so his rule might lenger have endurance.
First, to his gate he pointed a strong gard,
That none might enter but with issue hard:
Then, for the safegard of his personage,
He did appoint a warlike equipage
Of forreine beasts, not in the forest bred,
But part by land and part by water fed;
For tyrannie is with strange ayde supported.
Then unto him all monstrous beasts resorted
Bred of two kindes, as Griffons, Minotaures,
Crocodiles, Dragons, Beavers, and Centaures:
With those himselfe he strengthned mightelie,
That feare he neede no force of enemie.
Then gan he rule and tyrannize at will,
Like as the Foxe did guide his graceles skill,
And all wylde beasts mado vassals of his pleasures,
And with their spoyles enlarg'd his private treasures.
No care of justice, nor no rule of reason,
No temperance, nor no regard of season,
Did thenceforth ever enter in his minde,
But crueltie, the signe of currish kinde,
And sdeignfull pride, and wilfull arrogaunce;
Such followes those whom fortune doth advaunce.

But the false Foxe most kindly plaid his part:
For whatsoever mother wit or arte
Could worke, he put in proofe: no practise slie,
No counterpoint of cunning policie,
No reach, no breach, that might him profit bring,
But he the same did to his purpose wring.
Nought suffered he the Ape to give or graunt,
But through his hand must passe the fiaunt.
All offices, all leases by him lept,
And of them all whatso he likte he kept.
Justice he solde injustice for to buy,
And for to purchase for his progeny.
Ill might it prosper, that ill gotten was,
But, so he got it, little did he pas.
He fed his cubs with fat of all the soyle,
And with the sweete of others sweating toyle;
He crammed them with crumbs of benefices,
And fild their mouthes with meeds of malefices;
He cloathed them with all colours save white,
And loded them with lordships and with might,
So much as they were able well to beare,
That with the weight their backs nigh broken were.
He chaffred chayres in which churchmen were set,
And breach of lawes to privie ferme did let;
No statute so established might bee,
Nor ordinaunce so needfull, but that hee
Would violate, though not with violence,
Yet under colour of the confidence
The which the Ape reposd' in him alone,
And reckned him the kingdomes corner stone.
And ever, when he ought would bring to pas,
His long experience the platforme was:
And when he ought not pleasing would put by,
The cloke was care of thrift, and husbandry,
For to encrease the common treasures store.
But his owne treasure he encreased more,
And lifted up his loftie towres thereby,
That they began to threat the neighbour sky;
The whiles the princes pallaces fell fast
To ruine, (for what thing can ever last?)
And whilest the other peeres, for povertie,
Were forst their auncient houses to let lie,
And their olde castles to the ground to fall,
Which their forefathers, famous over all,
Had founded for the kingdomes ornament,
And for their memories long moniment.
But he no count made of nobilitie,
Nor the wilde beasts whom armes did glorifie,
The realmes chiefe strength and girlond of the crowne.
All these through fained crimes he thrust adowne,
Or made them dwell in darknes of disgrace:

For none but whom he list might come in place.
Of men of armes he had but small regard,
But kept them lowe, and streigned verie hard.
For men of learning little he esteemed;
His wisedome he above their learning deemed.
As for the rascall commons, least he cared;
For not so common was his bountie shared:
'Let God,' said he, 'if please, care for the manie,
I for my selfe must care before els anie.'
So did he good to none, to manie ill,
So did he all the kingdome rob and pill,
Yet none durst speake, ne none durst of him plaine;
So great he was in grace, and rich through gaine.
Ne would he anie let to have accesse
Unto the prince, but by his owne addresse:
For all that els did come were sure to faile;
Yet would he further none but for availe.
For on a time the Sheepe, to whom of yore
The Foxe had promised of friendship store,
What time the Ape the kingdome first did gaine,
Came to the court, her case there to complaine;
How that the Wolfe, her mortall enemie,
Had sithence slaine her lambe most cruellie;
And therefore crav'd to come unto the king,
To let him knowe the order of the thing.
'Soft, Gooddie Sheepe!' then said the Foxe, 'not soe:
Unto the king so rash ye may not goe;
He is with greater matter busied
Than a lambe, or the lambes owne mothers hed.
Ne certes may I take it well in part,
That ye my cousin Wolfe so fowly thwart,
And seeke with slaunder his good name to blot:
For there was cause, els doo it he would not:
Therefore surcease, good dame, and hence depart.'
So went the Sheepe away with heavie hart:
So manie moe, so everie one was used,
That to give largely to the boxe refused.
Now when high Jove, in whose almightie hand
The care of kings and power of empires stand,
Sitting one day within his turret hye,
From whence he vewes with his blacklidded eye
Whatso the heaven in his wide vawte containes,
And all that in the deepest earth remaines,
And troubled kingdome of wilde beasts behelde,
Whom not their kindly sovereigne did welde,
But an usurping Ape, with guile suborn'd,
Had all subverst, he sdeignfully it scorn'd
In his great heart, and hardly did refraine
But that with thunder bolts he had him slaine,
And driven downe to hell, his dewest meed.
But him avizing, he that dreadfull deed

Forbore, and rather chose with scornfull shame
Him to avenge, and blot his brutish name
Unto the world, that never after anie
Should of his race be voyd of infamie:
And his false counsellor, the cause of all,
To damne to death, or dole perpetuall,
From whence he never should be quit nor stal'd.
Forthwith he Mercurie unto him cal'd,
And bad him flie with never resting speed
Unto the forrest, where wilde beasts doo breed,
And there enquiring privily, to learne
What did of late chaunce to the Lyon stearne,
That he rul'd not the empire, as he ought;
And whence were all those plaints unto him brought
Of wrongs and spoyles by salvage beasts committed;
Which done, he bad the Lyon be remitted
Into his seate, and those same treachours vile
Be punished for their presumptuous guile.
The sonne of Maia, soone as he receiv'd
That word, streight with his azure wings he cleav'd
The liquid clowdes and lucid firmament;
Ne staid, till that he came with steep descent
Unto the place, where his prescript did showe.
There stouping, like an arrowe from a bowe,
He soft arrived on the grassie plaine,
And fairly paced forth with easie paine,
Till that unto the pallace nigh he came.
Then gan he to himselfe new shape to frame.
And that faire face, and that ambrosiall hew,
Which wonts to decke the gods immortall crew,
And beautefie the shinie firmament,
He doft, unfit for that rude rabblement.
So standing by the gates in strange disguize,
He gan enquire of some in secret wize,
Both of the king, and of his government,
And of the Foxe, and his false blandishment:
And evermore he heard each one complaine
Of foule abuses both in realme and raine:
Which yet to prove more true, he meant to see,
And an ey-witnes of each thing to bee.
Tho on his head his dreadfull hat he dight,
Which maketh him invisible in sight,
And mocketh th' eyes of all the lookers on,
Making them thinke it but a vision.
Through power of that, he runnes through enemies swerds;
Through power of that, he passeth through the herds
Of ravenous wilde beasts, and doth beguile
Their greedie mouthes of the expected spoyle;
Through power of that, his cunning theeveries
He wonts to worke, that none the same espies;
And through the power of that, he putteth on

What shape he list in apparition.
That on his head he wore, and in his hand
He tooke Caduceus, his snakie wand,
With which the damned ghosts he governeth,
And furies rules, and Tartare tempereth.
With that he causeth sleep to seize the eyes,
And feare the harts of all his enemyes;
And when him list, an universall night
Throughout the world he makes on everie wight,
As when his syre with Alcumena lay.
Thus dight, into the court he tooke his way,
Both through the gard, which never him descride,
And through the watchmen, who him never spide:
Thenceforth he past into each secrete part,
Whereas he saw, that sorely griev'd his hart,
Each place abounding with fowle injuries,
And fild with treasure rackt with robberies;
Each place defilde with blood of guiltles beasts,
Which had been slaine, to serve the Apes beheasts;
Gluttonie, malice, pride, and covetize,
And lawlesnes raigning with riotize;
Besides the infinite extortions,
Done through the Foxes great oppressions,
That the complaints thereof could not be tolde.
Which when he did with lothfull eyes beholde,
He would no more endure, but came his way,
And cast to seeke the Lion, where he may,
That he might worke the avengement for this shame
On those two caytives, which had bred him blame;
And seeking all the forrest busily,
At last he found where sleeping he did ly.
The wicked weed, which there the Foxe did lay,
From underneath his head he tooke away,
And then him waking, forced up to rize.
The Lion, looking up, gan him avize,
As one late in a traunce, what had of long
Become of him: for fantasie is strong.
'Arise,' said Mercurie, 'thou sluggish beast,
That here liest senseles, like the corpse deceast,
The whilste thy kingdome from thy head is rent,
And thy throne royall with dishonour blent:
Arise, and doo thy selfe redeeme from shame,
And be aveng'd on those that breed thy blame.'
Thereat enraged, soone he gan upstart,
Grinding his teeth, and grating his great hart,
And, rouzing up himselfe, for his rough hide
He gan to reach; but no where it espide.
Therewith he gan full terribly to rore,
And chafte at that indignitie right sore.
But when his crowne and scepter both he wanted,
Lord! how he fum'd, and sweld, and rag'd, and panted,

And threatned death and thousand deadly dolours
To them that had purloyn'd his princely honours!
With that in hast, disroabed as he was,
He toward his owne pallace forth did pas;
And all the way he roared as he went,
That all the forrest with astonishment
Thereof did tremble, and the beasts therein
Fled fast away from that so dreadfull din.
At last he came unto his mansion,
Where all the gates he found fast lockt anon,
And manie warders round about them stood:
With that he roar'd alowd, as he were wood,
That all the pallace quaked at the stound,
As if it quite were riven from the ground,
And all within were dead and hartles left;
And th' Ape himselfe, as one whose wits were reft,
Fled here and there, and everie corner sought,
To hide himselfe from his owne feared thought.
But the false Foxe, when he the Lion heard,
Fled closely forth, streightway of death afeard,
And to the Lion came, full lowly creeping,
With fained face, and watrie eyne halfe weeping,
T' excuse his former treason and abusion,
And turning all unto the Apes confusion:
Nath'les the royall beast forbore beleeving,
But bad him stay at ease till further preeving.
Then when he saw no entrance to him graunted,
Roaring yet lowder, that all harts it daunted,
Upon those gates with force he fiercely flewe,
And, rending them in pieces, felly slewe
Those warders strange, and all that els he met.
But th' Ape, still flying, he no where might get:
From rowme to rowme, from beame to beame he fled,
All breathles, and for feare now almost ded:
Yet him at last the Lyon spide, and caught,
And forth with shame unto his judgement brought.
Then all the beasts he causd' assembled bee,
To heare their doome, and sad ensample see:
The Foxe, first author of that treacherie,
He did uncase, and then away let flie.
But th' Apes long taile (which then he had) he quight
Cut off, and both eares pared of their hight;
Since which, all apes but halfe their eares have left,
And of their tailes are utterlie bereft.
So Mother Hubberd her discourse did end:
Which pardon me, if I amisse have pend,
For weake was my remembrance it to hold,
And bad her tongue, that it so bluntly tolde.

FINIS.

The Songe of Du Bellay, of which the 'Visions of Bellay' are a rendering, forms a kind of appendix to his Antiquitez de Rome. Spenser, having had his attention directed to the former, would naturally read also the latter: the result was this other translation, 'Ruins of Rome.' It is difficult to believe that this work is not also of his university days. In the 'Envoy,' to be sure, he refers to the Sepmaine of Du Bartas, first published in 1578, but the 'Envoy,' or that part of it, may very well be an afterthought. Both the weight of antecedent probability and the evidence of style would place the translation proper with the two earliest series of 'visions,' those of Bellay and of Petrarch. They are all three much of a piece. As translations in the larger sense, though often resourceful and apt, they can hardly be said to foretell the rare felicity of his later renderings from Tasso. As poetic exercises, however, they show at least the rudiments of that copious ease which is the mark of his maturer style.

I

Ye heavenly spirites, whose ashie cinders lie
Under deep ruines, with huge walls opprest,
But not your praise, the which shall never die,
Through your faire verses, ne in ashes rest;
If so be shrilling voyce of wight alive
May reach from hence to depth of darkest hell,
Then let those deep abysses open rive,
That ye may understand my shreiking yell.
Thrice having seene, under the heavens veale,
Your toombs devoted compasse over all,
Thrice unto you with lowd voyce I appeale,
And for your antique furie here doo call,
The whiles that I with sacred horror sing
Your glorie, fairest of all earthly thing.

II

Great Babylon her haughtie walls will praise,
And sharped steeples high shot up in ayre;
Greece will the olde Ephesian buildings blaze;
And Nylus nurslings their pyramides faire;
The same yet vaunting Greece will tell the storie
Of Joves great image in Olympus placed;
Mausolus worke will be the Carians glorie;
And Crete will boast the Labyrinth, now raced;
The antique Rhodian will likewise set forth
The great colosse, erect to Memorie;
And what els in the world is of like worth,
Some greater learned wit will magnifie.
But I will sing above all moniments
Seven Romane hils, the worlds seven wonderments.

III

Thou stranger, which for Rome in Rome here seekest,

And nought of Rome in Rome perceiv'st at all,
These same olde walls, olde arches, which thou seest,
Olde palaces, is that which Rome men call.
Behold what wreake, what ruine, and what wast,
And how that she, which with her mightie powre
Tam'd all the world, hath tam'd herselfe at last,
The pray of Time, which all things doth devowre.
Rome now of Rome is th' onely funerall,
And onely Rome of Rome hath victorie;
Ne ought save Tyber hastning to his fall
Remaines of all: O worlds inconstancie!
That which is firme doth flit and fall away,
And that is flitting doth abide and stay.

IV
She, whose high top above the starres did sore,
One foote on Thetis, th' other on the Morning,
One hand on Scythia, th' other on the More,
Both heaven and earth in roundnesse compassing,
Jove, fearing least, if she should greater growe,
The old giants should once againe uprise,
Her whelm'd with hills, these seven hils, which be nowe
Tombes of her greatnes, which did threate the skies:
Upon her head he heapt Mount Saturnal,
Upon her bellie th' antique Palatine,
Upon her stomacke laid Mount Quirinal,
On her left hand the noysome Esquiline,
And Cælian on the right; but both her feete
Mount Viminal and Aventine doo meete.

V
Who lists to see what ever nature, arte,
And heaven could doo, O Rome, thee let him see,
In case thy greatnes he can gesse in harte
By that which but the picture is of thee.
Rome is no more: but if the shade of Rome
May of the bodie yeeld a seeming sight,
It 's like a corse drawne forth out of the tombe
By magicke skill out of eternall night:
The corpes of Rome in ashes is entombed,
And her great spirite, rejoyned to the spirite
Of this great masse, is in the same enwombed;
But her brave writings, which her famous merite,
In spight of Time, out of the dust doth reare,
Doo make her idole through the world appeare.

VI
Such as the Berecynthian goddesse bright,
In her swift charret with high turrets crownde,
Proud that so manie gods she brought to light,
Such was this citie in her good daies fownd:

This citie, more than that great Phrygian mother
Renowm'd for fruite of famous progenie,
Whose greatnes by the greatnes of none other,
But by her selfe, her equall match could see:
Rome onely might to Rome compared bee,
And onely Rome could make great Rome to tremble:
So did the gods by heavenly doome deeree,
That other earthlie power should not resemble
Her that did match the whole earths puissaunce,
And did her courage to the heavens advaunce.

VII
Ye sacred ruines, and ye tragick sights,
Which onely doo the name of Rome retaine,
Olde moniments, which of so famous sprights
The honour yet in ashes doo maintaine,
Triumphant arcks, spyres neighbours to the skie,
That you to see doth th' heaven it selfe appall,
Alas! by little ye to nothing flie,
The peoples fable, and the spoyle of all:
And though your frames do for a time make warre
Gainst Time, yet Time in time shall ruinate
Your workes and names, and your last reliques marre.
My sad desires, rest therefore moderate:
For if that Time make ende of things so sure,
It als will end the paine which I endure.

VIII
Through armes and vassals Rome the world subdu'd,
That one would weene that one sole cities strength
Both land and sea in roundnes had survew'd,
To be the measure of her bredth and length:
This peoples vertue yet so fruitfull was
Of vertuous nephewes, that posteritie,
Striving in power their grandfathers to passe,
The lowest earth join'd to the heaven hie;
To th' end that, having all parts in their power,
Nought from the Romane Empire might be quight;
And that though Time doth commonwealths devowre,
Yet no time should so low embase their hight,
That her head, earth'd in her foundations deep,
Should not her name and endles honour keep.

IX
Ye cruell starres, and eke ye gods unkinde,
Heaven envious, and bitter stepdame Nature,
Be it by fortune, or by course of kinde,
That ye doo weld th' affaires of earthlie creature;
Why have your hands long sithence traveiled
To frame this world, that doth endure so long?
Or why were not these Romane palaces

Made of some matter no lesse firme and strong?
I say not, as the common voyce doth say,
That all things which beneath the moone have being
Are temporall, and subject to decay:
But I say rather, though not all agreeing
With some that weene the contrarie in thought,
That all this whole shall one day come to nought.

X

As that brave sonne of Aeson, which by charmes
Atcheiv'd the golden fleece in Colchid land,
Out of the earth engendred men of armes
Of dragons teeth, sowne in the sacred sand;
So this brave towne, that in her youthlie daies
An hydra was of warriours glorious,
Did fill with her renowmed nourslings praise
The firie sunnes both one and other hous:
But they at last, there being then not living
An Hercules, so ranke seed to represse,
Emongst themselves with cruell furie striving,
Mow'd downe themselves with slaughter mercilesse;
Renewing in themselves that rage unkinde,
Which whilom did those earthborn brethren blinde.

XI

Mars, shaming to have given so great head
To his off-spring, that mortall puissaunce,
Puft up with pride of Romane hardie-head,
Seem'd above heavens powre it selfe to advaunce,
Cooling againe his former kindled heate,
With which he had those Romane spirits fild,
Did blowe new fire, and with enflamed breath
Into the Gothicke colde hot rage instil'd:
Then gan that nation, th' earths new giant brood,
To dart abroad the thunder bolts of warre,
And, beating downe these walls with furious mood
Into her mothers bosome, all did marre;
To th' end that none, all were it Jove his sire,
Should boast himselfe of the Romane Empire.

XII

Like as whilome the children of the earth
Heapt hils on hils, to scale the starrie skie,
And fight against the gods of heavenly berth,
Whiles Jove at them his thunderbolts let flie;
All suddenly with lightning overthrowne,
The furious squadrons downe to ground did fall,
That th' earth under her childrens weight did grone,
And th' heavens in glorie triumpht over all:
So did that haughtie front, which heaped was
On these seven Romane hils, it selfe upreare

Over the world, and lift her loftie face
Against the heaven, that gan her force to feare.
But now these scorned fields bemone her fall,
And gods secure feare not her force at all.

XIII
Nor the swift furie of the flames aspiring,
Nor the deep wounds of victours raging blade,
Nor ruthlesse spoyle of souldiers blood-desiring,
The which so oft thee (Rome) their conquest made;
Ne stroke on stroke of fortune variable,
Ne rust of age hating continuance,
Nor wrath of gods, nor spight of men unstable,
Nor thou opposd' against thine owne puissance;
Nor th' horrible uprore of windes high blowing,
Nor swelling streames of that god snakie-paced,
Which hath so often with his overflowing
Thee drenched, have thy pride so much abaced,
But that this nothing, which they have thee left,
Makes the world wonder what they from thee reft.

XIV
As men in summer fearles passe the foord,
Which is in winter lord of all the plaine,
And with his tumbling streames doth beare aboord
The ploughmans hope and shepheards labour vaine:
And as the coward beasts use to despise
The noble lion after his lives end,
Whetting their teeth, and with vaine foolhardise
Daring the foe, that cannot him defend:
And as at Troy most dastards of the Greekes
Did brave about the corpes of Hector colde;
So those which whilome wont with pallid cheekes
The Romane triumphs glorie to behold,
Now on these ashie tombes shew boldnesse vaine,
And, conquer'd, dare the conquerour disdaine.

XV
Ye pallid spirits, and ye ashie ghoasts,
Which, joying in the brightnes of your day,
Brought foorth those signes of your presumptuous boasts
Which now their dusty reliques do bewray;
Tell me, ye spirits (sith the darksome river
Of Styx, not passable to soules returning,
Enclosing you in thrice three wards for ever,
Doo not restraine your images still mourning)
Tell me then (for perhaps some one of you
Yet here above him secretly doth hide)
Doo ye not feele your torments to accrewe,
When ye sometimes behold the ruin'd pride
Of these old Romane works, built with your hands,

To have become nought els but heaped sands?

XVI

Like as ye see the wrathfull sea from farre,
In a great mountaine heap't with hideous noyse,
Eftsoones of thousand billowes shouldred narre,
Against a rocke to breake with dreadfull poyse:
Like as ye see fell Boreas with sharpe blast,
Tossing huge tempests through the troubled skie,
Eftsoones having his wide wings spent in wast,
To stop his wearie cariere suddenly:
And as ye see huge flames spred diverslie,
Gathered in one up to the heavens to spyre,
Eftsoones consum'd to fall downe feebily:
So whilom did this monarchie aspyre
As waves, as winde, as fire spred over all,
Till it by fatall doome adowne did fall.

XVII

So long as Joves great bird did make his flight,
Bearing the fire with which heaven doth us fray,
Heaven had not feare of that presumptuous might,
With which the giaunts did the gods assay.
But all so soone as scortching sunne had brent
His wings, which wont the earth to overspredd,
The earth out of her massie wombe forth sent
That antique horror, which made heaven adredd.
Then was the Germane raven in disguise
That Romane eagle seene to cleave asunder,
And towards heaven freshly to arise
Out of these mountaines, now consum'd to pouder:
In which the foule that serves to beare the lightning
Is now no more seen flying, nor alighting.

XVIII

These heapes of stones, these old wals which ye see,
Were first enclosures but of salvage soyle;
And these brave pallaces, which maystred bee
Of Time, were shepheards cottages some-while.
Then tooke the shepheards kingly ornaments,
And the stout hynde arm'd his right hand with steele:
Eftsoones their rule of yearely presidents
Grew great, and six months greater a great deele;
Which, made perpetuall, rose to so great might,
That thence th' imperiall eagle rooting tooke,
Till th' heaven it selfe, opposing gainst her might,
Her power to Peters successor betooke;
Who, shepheardlike, (as Fates the same foreseeing)
Doth shew that all things turne to their first being.

XIX

All that is perfect, which th' heaven beautefies;
All that 's imperfect, borne belowe the moone;
All that doth feede our spirits and our eies;
And all that doth consume our pleasures soone;
All the mishap, the which our daies out-weares;
All the good hap of th' oldest times afore,
Rome in the time of her great ancesters,
Like a Pandora, locked long in store.
But destinie this huge chaos turmoyling,
In which all good and evill was enclosed,
Their heavenly vertues from these woes assoyling,
Caried to heaven, from sinfull bondage losed:
But their great sinnes, the causers of their paine,
Under these antique ruines yet remaine.

XX
No otherwise than raynie cloud, first fed
With earthly vapours gathered in the ayre,
Eftsoones in compas arch't, to steepe his hed,
Doth plonge himselfe in Tethys bosome faire;
And mounting up againe, from whence he came,
With his great bellie spreds the dimmed world,
Till at the last, dissolving his moist frame,
In raine, or snowe, or haile he forth is horld;
This citie, which was first but shepheards shade,
Uprising by degrees, grewe to such height,
That queene of land and sea her selfe she made.
At last, not able to beare so great weight,
Her power, disperst, through all the world did vade;
To shew that all in th' end to nought shall fade.

XXI
The same which Pyrrhus and the puissunce
Of Afrike could not tame, that same brave citie,
Which, with stout courage arm'd against mischaunce,
Sustein'd the shocke of common enmitie;
Long as her ship, tost with so manie freakes,
Had all the world in armes against her bent,
Was never seene that anie fortunes wreakes
Could breake her course begun with brave intent.
But when the object of her vertue failed,
Her power it selfe against it selfe did arme;
As he that having long in tempest sailed,
Faine would arive, but cannot for the storme,
If too great winde against the port him drive,
Doth in the port it selfe his vessell rive.

XXII
When that brave honour of the Latine name,
Which mear'd her rule with Africa and Byze,
With Thames inhabitants of noble fame,

And they which see the dawning day arize,
Her nourslings did with mutinous uprore
Harten against her selfe, her conquer'd spoile,
Which she had wonne from all the world afore,
Of all the world was spoyl'd within a while.
So, when the compast course of the universe
In six and thirtie thousand yeares is ronne,
The bands of th' elements shall backe reverse
To their first discord, and be quite undonne:
The seedes, of which all things at first were bred,
Shall in great Chaos wombe againe be hid.

XXIII
O warie wisedome of the man that would
That Carthage towres from spoile should be forborne,
To th' end that his victorious people should
With cancring laisure not be overworne!
He well foresaw, how that the Romane courage,
Impatient of pleasures faint desires,
Through idlenes would turne to civill rage,
And be her selfe the matter of her fires.
For in a people given all to ease,
Ambition is engendred easily;
As in a vicious bodie, grose disease
Soone growes through humours superfluitie.
That came to passe, when, swolne with plenties pride,
Nor prince, nor peere, nor kin, they would abide.

XXIV
If the blinde Furie, which warres breedeth oft,
Wonts not t' enrage the hearts of equall beasts,
Whether they fare on foote, or flie aloft,
Or armed be with clawes, or scalie creasts,
What fell Erynnis, with hot burning tongs,
Did grype your hearts, with noysome rage imbew'd,
That, each to other working cruell wrongs,
Your blades in your owne bowels you embrew'd?
Was this, ye Romanes, your hard destinie?
Or some old sinne, whose unappeased guilt
Powr'd vengeance forth on you eternallie?
Or brothers blood, the which at first was spilt
Upon your walls, that God might not endure
Upon the same to set foundation sure?

XXV
O that I had the Thracian poets harpe,
For to awake out of th' infernall shade
Those antique Cæsars, sleeping long in darke,
The which this auncient citie whilome made!
Or that I had Amphions instrument,
To quicken with his vitall notes accord

The stonie joynts of these old walls now rent,
By which th' Ausonian light might be restor'd!
Or that at least I could with pencill fine
Fashion the pourtraicts of these palacis,
By paterne of great Virgils spirit divine!
I would assay with that which in me is
To builde, with levell of my loftie style,
That which no hands can evermore compyle.

XXVI

Who list the Romane greatnes forth to figure,
Him needeth not to seeke for usage right
Of line, or lead, or rule, or squaire, to measure
Her length, her breadth, her deepnes, or her hight;
But him behooves to vew in compasse round
All that the ocean graspes in his long armes;
Be it where the yerely starre doth scortch the ground,
Or where colde Boreas blowes his bitter stormes.
Rome was th' whole world, and al the world was Rome,
And if things nam'd their names doo equalize,
When land and sea ye name, then name ye Rome,
And naming Rome, ye land and sea comprize:
For th' auncient plot of Rome, displayed plaine,
The map of all the wide world doth containe.

XXVII

Thou that at Rome astonisht dost behold
The antique pride, which menaced the skie,
These haughtie heapes, these palaces of olde,
These wals, these arcks, these baths, these temples hie,
Judge, by these ample ruines vew, the rest
The which injurious time hath quite outworne,
Since, of all workmen helde in reckning best,
Yet these olde fragments are for paternes borne:
Then also marke, how Rome, from day to day,
Repayring her decayed fashion,
Renewes herselfe with buildings rich and gay;
That one would judge that the Romaine Dæmon
Doth yet himselfe with fatall hand enforce,
Againe on foote to reare her pouldred corse.

XXVIII

He that hath seene a great oke drie and dead,
Yet clad with reliques of some trophees olde,
Lifting to heaven her aged hoarie head,
Whose foote in ground hath left but feeble holde,
But halfe disbowel'd lies above the ground,
Shewing her wreathed rootes, and naked armes,
And on her trunke, all rotten and unsound,
Onely supports herselfe for meate of wormes,
And though she owe her fall to the first winde,

Yet of the devout people is ador'd,
And manie yong plants spring out of her rinde;
Who such an oke hath seene, let him record
That such this cities honour was of yore,
And mongst all cities florished much more.

XXIX
All that which Aegypt whilome did devise,
All that which Greece their temples to embrave,
After th' Ionicke, Atticke, Doricke guise,
Or Corinth skil'd in curious workes to grave,
All that Lysippus practike arte could forme,
Apelles wit, or Phidias his skill,
Was wont this auncient citie to adorne,
And the heaven it selfe with her wide wonders fill.
All that which Athens ever brought forth wise,
All that which Afrike ever brought forth strange,
All that which Asie ever had of prise,
Was here to see. O mervelous great change!
Rome, living, was the worlds sole ornament,
And dead, is now the worlds sole moniment.

XXX
Like as the seeded field greene grasse first showes,
Then from greene grasse into a stalke doth spring,
And from a stalke into an eare forthgrowes,
Which eare the frutefull graine doth shortly bring;
And as in season due the husband mowes
The waving lockes of those faire yeallow heares,
Which, bound in sheaves, and layd in comely rowes,
Upon the naked fields in stackes he reares:
So grew the Romane Empire by degree,
Till that barbarian hands it quite did spill,
And left of it but these olde markes to see,
Of which all passers by doo somewhat pill,
As they which gleane, the reliques use to gather,
Which th' husbandman behind him chanst to scater.

XXXI
That same is now nought but a champianwide,
Where all this worlds pride once was situate.
No blame to thee, whosoever dost abide
By Nyle, or Gange, or Tygre, or Euphrate;
Ne Afrike thereof guiltie is, nor Spaine,
Nor the bolde people by the Thamis brincks,
Nor the brave warlicke brood of Alemaine,
Nor the borne souldier which Rhine running drinks.
Thou onely cause, O Civill Furie, art:
Which, sowing in th' Aemathian fields thy spight,
Didst arme thy hand against thy proper hart;
To th' end that when thou wast in greatest hight

To greatnes growne, through long prosperitie,
Thou then adowne might'st fall more horriblie.

XXXII
Hope ye, my verses, that posteritie
Of age ensuing shall you ever read?
Hope ye that ever immortalitie
So meane harpes worke may chalenge for her meed?
If under heaven anie endurance were,
These moniments, which not in paper writ,
But in porphyre and marble doo appeare,
Might well have hop'd to have obtained it.
Nath'les, my lute, whom Phoebus deigned to give,
Cease not to sound these olde antiquities:
For if that Time doo let thy glorie live,
Well maist thou boast, how ever base thou bee,
That thou art first which of thy nation song
Th' olde honour of the people gowned long.

L'ENVOY
Bellay, first garland of free poësie
That France brought forth, though fruitfull of brave wits,
Well worthie thou of immortalitie,
That long hast traveld by thy learned writs,
Olde Rome out of her ashes to revive,
And give a second life to dead decayes:
Needes must he all eternitie survive,
That can to other give eternall dayes.
Thy dayes therefore are endles, and thy prayse
Excelling all that ever went before;
And, after thee, gins Bartas hie to rayse
His heavenly Muse, th' Almightie to adore.
Live happie spirits, th' honour of your name,
And fill the world with never dying fame.

FINIS.

MUIOPOTMOS, or THE FATE OF THE BUTTERFLIE - DEDICATED TO THE MOST FAIRE AND
VERTUOUS LADIE: THE LADIE CAREY

TO THE RIGHT WORTHY AND VERTUOUS LADIE; THE LADIE CAREY

Most brave and bountifull Lady: for so excellent favours as I have received at your sweet handes, to
offer these fewe leaves as in recompence, should be as to offer flowers to the gods for their divine
benefites. Therefore I have determined to give my selfewholy to you, as quite abandoned from my
selfe, and absolutely vowed to your services: which in all right is ever held for full recompence of
debt or damage to have the person yeelded. My person I wot wel how little worth it is. But the
faithfull minde and humble zeale which I beare unto your Ladiship may perhaps be more of price, as
may please you to account and use the poore service thereof; which taketh glory to advance your

excellent partes and noble vertues, and to spend it selfe in honouring you: not so much for your great bounty to my self, which yet may not be unminded; nor for name or kindrerds sake by you vouchsafed, beeing also regardable; as for that honorable name, which yee have by your brave deserts purchast to your self, and spred in the mouths of al men: with which I have also presumed to grace my verses, and under your name to commend to the world this smal poeme; the which beseeching your Ladiship to take in worth, and of all things therein according to your wonted graciousnes to make a milde construction, I humbly pray for your happines.
Your Ladiships ever
humbly;

Edmund Spenser

'Muiopotmos' cannot be dated with certainty. In style it would seem to be more mature than the work of the Calendar period; it may have been written in Ireland; one rather associates it with that period of delight in London while the poet was seeing his Faery Queen through the press. If the date upon its separate title page is to be trusted, it must have been written, at latest, not long after his arrival in England.

By contrast to the motley and impressive mediævalism of 'Mother Hubberd's Tale,' this poem would seem to be conspicuously Renaissance Italian. Its subject is a mere nothing: it tells no story that could not be told in full in a stanza, it presents no situation for the delicate rhetoric of the emotions: it is a mere running frieze of images and scenes, linked in fanciful continuity. It is organized as a mockheroic poem, but its appeal is essentially to the eye. Myths, invented or real, that seem to form themselves spontaneously into pictures, the landscape of the gardens, fantastic armor, the figured scenes of tapestry richly bordered, these are of a poetry akin to the plastic arts, such as one finds in the Stanze of Poliziano. Yet the temper of 'Muiopotmos' is not that of the Stanza and their like. It is rather of the air than of the earth. One might think it an emanation of the theme itself and fancy that the frail wings of the butterfly had been spread for the style, delicately colored, ethereal. The poet of the Faery Queen never more happily escaped into 'delight with liberty' than here.

MUIOPOTMOS or THE FATE OF THE BUTTERFLIE

I sing of deadly dolorous debate,
Stir'd up through wrathfull Nemesis despight,
Betwixt two mightie ones of great estate,
Drawne into armes, and proofe of mortall fight,
Through prowd ambition and hartswelling hate,
Whilest neither could the others greater might
And sdeignfull scorne endure; that from small jarre
Their wraths at length broke into open warre.

The roote whereof and tragicall effect,
Vouchsafe, O thou the mournfulst Muse of nyne,
That wontst the tragick stage for to direct,
In funerall complaints and waylfull tyne,
Reveale to me, and all the meanes detect
Through which sad Clarion did at last declyne
To lowest wretchednes: And is there then

Such rancour in the harts of mightie men?

Of all the race of silver-winged flies
Which doo possesse the empire of the aire,
Betwixt the centred earth and azure skies,
Was none more favourable, nor more faire,
Whilst heaven did favour his felicities,
Then Clarion, the eldest sonne and haire
Of Muscaroll, and in his fathers sight
Of all alive did seeme the fairest wight.

With fruitfull hope his aged breast he fed
Of future good, which his yong toward yeares,
Full of brave courage and bold hardyhed,
Above th' ensample of his equall peares,
Did largely promise, and to him forered
(Whilst oft his heart did melt in tender teares)
That he in time would sure prove such an one,
As should be worthie of his fathers throne.

The fresh yong flie, in whom the kindly fire
Of lustfull yongth began to kindle fast,
Did much disdaine to subject his desire
To loathsome sloth, or houres in ease to wast,
But joy'd to range abroad in fresh attire,
Through the wide compas of the ayrie coast,
And with unwearied wings each part t' inquire
Of the wide rule of his renowmed sire.

For he so swift and nimble was of flight,
That from this lower tract he dar'd to stie
Up to the clowdes, and thence, with pineons light,
To mount aloft unto the christall skie,
To vew the workmanship of heavens hight:
Whence downe descending he along would flie
Upon the streaming rivers, sport to finde;
And oft would dare to tempt the troublous winde.

So on a summers day, when season milde
With gentle calme the world had quieted,
And high in heaven Hyperions fierie childe
Ascending, did his beames abroad dispred,
Whiles all the heavens on lower creatures smilde,
Yong Clarion, with vauntfull lustiehead,
After his guize did cast abroad to fare,
And theretoo gan his furnitures prepare.

His breastplate first, that was of substance pure,
Before his noble heart he firmely bound,
That mought his life from yron death assure,
And ward his gentle corpes from cruell wound:

For it by arte was framed to endure
The bit of balefull steele and bitter stownd,
No lesse than that which Vulcane made to sheild
Achilles life from fate of Troyan field.

And then about his shoulders broad he threw
An hairie hide of some wilde beast, whom hee
In salvage forrest by adventure slew,
And reft the spoyle his ornament to bee:
Which, spreadding all his backe with dreadfull vew,
Made all that him so horrible did see
Thinke him Alcides with the lyons skin,
When the Næmean conquest he did win.

Upon his head, his glistering burganet,
The which was wrought by wonderous device,
And curiously engraven, he did set:
The mettall was of rare and passing price;
Not Bilbo steele, nor brasse from Corinth fet,
Nor costly oricalche from strange Phœnice;
But such as could both Phœbus arrowes ward,
And th' hayling darts of heaven beating hard.

Therein two deadly weapons fixt he bore,
Strongly outlaunced towards either side,
Like two sharpe speares, his enemies to gore:
Like as a warlike brigandine, applyde
To fight, layes forth her threatfull pikes afore,
The engines which in them sad death doo hyde:
So did this flie outstretch his fearefull hornes,
Yet so as him their terrour more adornes.

Lastly his shinie wings, as silver bright,
Painted with thousand colours, passing farre
All painters skill, he did about him dight:
Not halfe so manie sundrie colours arre
In Iris bowe, ne heaven doth shine so bright,
Distinguished with manie a twinckling starre,
Nor Junoes bird in her ey-spotted traine
So manie goodly colours doth containe.

Ne (may it be withouten perill spoken)
The Archer god, the sonne of Cytheree,
That joyes on wretched lovers to be wroken,
And heaped spoyles of bleeding harts to see,
Beares in his wings so manie a changefull token.
Ah! my liege lord, forgive it unto mee,
If ought against thine honour I have tolde;
Yet sure those wings were fairer manifolde.

Full manie a ladie faire, in court full oft

Beholding them, him secretly envide,
And wisht that two such fannes, so silken soft
And golden faire, her love would her provide;
Or that, when them the gorgeous flie had doft,
Some one, that would with grace be gratifide,
From him would steale them privily away,
And bring to her so precious a pray.

Report is that Dame Venus on a day,
In spring when flowres doo clothe the fruitful ground,
Walking abroad with all her nymphes to play,
Bad her faire damzels, flocking her arownd,
To gather flowres, her forhead to array.
Emongst the rest a gentle nymph was found,
Hight Astery, excelling all the crewe
In curteous usage and unstained hewe.

Who, being nimbler joynted than the rest,
And more industrious, gathered more store
Of the fields honour than the others best;
Which they in secret harts envying sore,
Tolde Venus, when her as the worthiest
She praisd', that Cupide (as they heard before)
Did lend her secret aide in gathering
Into her lap the children of the Spring.

Whereof the goddesse gathering jealous feare,
Not yet unmindfull how not long agoe
Her sonne to Psyche secrete love did beare,
And long it close conceal'd, till mickle woe
Thereof arose, and manie a rufull teare,
Reason with sudden rage did overgoe,
And giving hastie credit to th' accuser,
Was led away of them that did abuse her.

Eftsoones that damzel, by her heavenly might,
She turn'd into a winged butterflie,
In the wide aire to make her wandring flight;
And all those flowres, with which so plenteouslie
Her lap she filled had, that bred her spight,
She placed in her wings, for memorie
Of her pretended crime, though crime none were:
Since which that flie them in her wings doth beare.

Thus the fresh Clarion, being readie dight,
Unto his journey did himselfe addresse,
And with good speed began to take his flight:
Over the fields, in his franke lustinesse,
And all the champion he soared light,
And all the countrey wide he did possesse,
Feeding upon their pleasures bounteouslie,

That none gainsaid, nor none did him envie.

The woods, the rivers, and the medowes green,
With his aire-cutting wings he measured wide,
Ne did he leave the mountaines bare unseene,
Nor the ranke grassie fennes delights untride.
But none of these, how ever sweete they beene,
Most please his fancie, nor him cause t' abide:
His choicefull sense with everie change doth flit;
No common things may please a wavering wit.

To the gay gardins his unstaid desire
Him wholly caried, to refresh his sprights:
There lavish Nature, in her best attire,
Powres forth sweete odors, and alluring sights;
And Arte, with her contending, doth aspire
T' excell the naturall with made delights:
And all that faire or pleasant may be found
In riotous excesse doth there abound.

There he arriving, round about doth flie,
From bed to bed, from one to other border,
And takes survey, with curious busie eye,
Of everie flowre and herbe there set in order;
Now this, now that, he tasteth tenderly,
Yet none of them he rudely doth disorder,
Ne with his feete their silken leaves deface;
But pastures on the pleasures of each place.

And evermore with most varietie,
And change of sweetnesse (for all change is sweete)
He casts his glutton sense to satisfie;
Now sucking of the sap of herbe most meete,
Or of the deaw, which yet on them does lie,
Now in the same bathing his tender feete:
And then he pearcheth on some braunch thereby,
To weather him, and his moyst wings to dry.

And then againe he turneth to his play,
To spoyle the pleasures of that paradise:
The wholsome saulge, and lavender still gray,
Ranke smelling rue, and cummin good for eyes,
The roses raigning in the pride of May,
Sharpe isope, good for greene wounds remedies,
Faire marigoldes, and bees-alluring thime,
Sweete marjoram, and daysies decking prime:

Coole violets, and orpine growing still,
Embathed balme, and chearfull galingale,
Fresh costmarie, and breathfull camomill,
Dull poppie, and drink-quickning setuale,

Veyne-healing verven, and hed-purging dill,
Sound savorie, and bazill hartie-hale,
Fat colworts, and comforting perseline,
Colde lettuce, and refreshing rosmarine.

And whatso else of vertue good or ill
Grewe in this gardin, fetcht from farre away,
Of everie one he takes, and tastes at will,
And on their pleasures greedily doth pray.
Then, when he hath both plaid, and fed his fill,
In the warme sunne he doth himselfe embay,
And there him rests in riotous suffisaunce
Of all his gladfulnes and kingly joyaunce.

What more felicitie can fall to creature
Than to enjoy delight with libertie,
And to be lord of all the workes of Nature,
To raine in th' aire from earth to highest skie,
To feed on flowres and weeds of glorious feature,
To take what ever thing doth please the eie?
Who rests not pleased with such happines,
Well worthie he to taste of wretchednes.

But what on earth can long abide in state,
Or who can him assure of happie day;
Sith morning faire may bring fowle evening late,
And least mishap the most blisse alter may?
For thousand perills lie in close awaite
About us daylie, to worke our decay;
That none, except a God, or God him guide,
May them avoyde, or remedie provide.

And whatso heavens in their secret doome
Ordained have, how can fraile fleshly wight
Forecast, but it must needs to issue come?
The sea, the aire, the fire, the day, the night,
And th' armies of their creatures all and some
Do serve to them, and with importune might
Warre against us, the vassals of their will.
Who then can save what they dispose to spill?

Not thou, O Clarion, though fairest thou
Of all thy kinde, unhappie happie flie,
Whose cruell fate is woven even now
Of Joves owne hand, to worke thy miserie:
Ne may thee helpe the manie hartie vow,
Which thy olde sire with sacred pietie
Hath powred forth for thee, and th' altars sprent:
Nought may thee save from heavens avengement.

It fortuned (as heavens had behight)

That in this gardin, where yong Clarion
Was wont to solace him, a wicked wight,
The foe of faire things, th' author of confusion,
The shame of Nature, the bondslave of spight,
Had lately built his hatefull mansion,
And, lurking closely, in awayte now lay,
How he might anie in his trap betray.

But when he spide the joyous butterflie
In this faire plot dispacing too and fro,
Fearles of foes and hidden jeopardie,
Lord! how he gan for to bestirre him tho,
And to his wicked worke each part applie!
His heart did earne against his hated foe,
And bowels so with ranckling poyson swelde,
That scarce the skin the strong contagion helde.

The cause why he this flie so maliced
Was (as in stories it is written found)
For that his mother which him bore and bred,
The most fine-fingred workwoman on ground,
Arachne, by his meanes was vanquished
Of Pallas, and in her owne skill confound,
When she with her for excellence contended,
That wrought her shame, and sorrow never ended.

For the Tritonian goddesse, having hard
Her blazed fame, which all the world had fil'd,
Came downe to prove the truth, and due reward
For her prais-worthie workmanship to yeild:
But the presumptuous damzel rashly dar'd
The goddesse selfe to chalenge to the field,
And to compare with her in curious skill
Of workes with loome, with needle, and with quill.

Minerva did the chalenge not refuse,
But deign'd with her the paragon to make:
So to their worke they sit, and each doth chuse
What storie she will for her tapet take.
Arachne figur'd how Jove did abuse
Europa like a bull, and on his backe
Her through the sea did beare; so lively seene,
That it true sea and true bull ye would weene.

She seem'd still backe unto the land to looke,
And her play-fellowes aide to call, and feare
The dashing of the waves, that up she tooke
Her daintie feete, and garments gathered neare:
But (Lord!) how she in everie member shooke,
When as the land she saw no more appeare,
But a wilde wildernes of waters deepe!

Then gan she greatly to lament and weepe.

Before the bull she pictur'd winged Love,
With his yong brother Sport, light fluttering
Upon the waves, as each had been a dove;
The one his bowe and shafts, the other spring
A burning teade about his head did move,
As in their syres new love both triumphing:
And manie Nymphes about them flocking round,
And manie Tritons, which their hornes did sound.

And round about, her worke she did empale
With a faire border wrought of sundrie flowres,
Enwoven with an yvie winding trayle:
A goodly worke, full fit for kingly bowres,
Such as Dame Pallas, such as Envie pale,
That al good things with venemous tooth devowres,
Could not accuse. Then gan the goddesse bright
Her selfe likewise unto her worke to dight.

She made the storie of the olde debate,
Which she with Neptune did for Athens trie:
Twelve gods doo sit around in royall state,
And Jove in midst with awfull majestie,
To judge the strife betweene them stirred late:
Each of the gods by his like visnomie
Eathe to be knowen; but Jove above them all,
By his great lookes and power imperiall.

Before them stands the god of seas in place,
Clayming that sea-coast citie as his right,
And strikes the rockes with his three-forked mace;
Whenceforth issues a warlike steed in sight,
The signe by which he chalengeth the place;
That all the gods, which saw his wondrous might,
Did surely deeme the victorie his due:
But seldome seene, forejudgement proveth true.

Then to her selfe she gives her Aegide shield,
And steelhed speare, and morion on her hedd,
Such as she oft is seene in warlicke field:
Then sets she forth, how with her weapon dredd
She smote the ground, the which streight foorth did yield
A fruitfull olyve tree, with berries spredd,
That all the gods admir'd; then all the storie
She compast with a wreathe of olyves hoarie.

Emongst those leaves she made a butterflie,
With excellent device and wondrous slight,
Fluttring among the olives wantonly,
That seem'd to live, so like it was in sight:

The velvet nap which on his wings doth lie,
The silken downe with which his backe is dight,
His broad outstretched hornes, his hayrie thies,
His glorious colours, and his glistering eies.

Which when Arachne saw, as overlaid
And mastered with workmanship so rare,
She stood astonied long, ne ought gainesaid,
And with fast fixed eyes on her did stare,
And by her silence, signe of one dismaid,
The victorie did yeeld her as her share:
Yet did she inly fret, and felly burne,
And all her blood to poysonous rancor turne:

That shortly from the shape of womanhed,
Such as she was, when Pallas she attempted,
She grew to hideous shape of dryrihed,
Pined with griefe of follie late repented:
Eftsoones her white streight legs were altered
To crooked crawling shankes, of marrowe empted,
And her faire face to fowle and loathsome hewe,
And her fine corpes to a bag of venim grewe.

This cursed creature, mindfull of that olde
Enfested grudge, the which his mother felt,
So soone as Clarion he did beholde,
His heart with vengefull malice inly swelt;
And weaving straight a net with manie a folde
About the cave in which he lurking dwelt,
With fine small cords about it stretched wide,
So finely sponne that scarce they could be spide.

Not anie damzell, which her vaunteth most
In skilfull knitting of soft silken twyne;
Nor anie weaver, which his worke doth boast
In dieper, in damaske, or in lyne;
Nor anie skil'd in workmanship embost;
Nor anie skil'd in loupes of fingring fine,
Might in their divers cunning ever dare,
With this so curious networke to compare.

Ne doo I thinke that that same subtil gin,
The which the Lemnian god framde craftilie,
Mars sleeping with his wife to compasse in,
That all the gods with common mockerie
Might laugh at them, and scorne their shamefull sin,
Was like to this. This same he did applie
For to entrap the careles Clarion,
That rang'd each where without suspition.

Suspition of friend, nor feare of foe,

That hazarded his health, had he at all,
But walkt at will, and wandred too and fro,
In the pride of his freedome principall:
Litle wist he his fatall future woe,
But was secure; the liker he to fall.
He likest is to fall into mischaunce,
That is regardles of his governaunce.

Yet still Aragnoll (so his foe was hight)
Lay lurking covertly him to surprise,
And all his gins, that him entangle might,
Drest in good order as he could devise.
At length the foolish flie, without foresight,
As he that did all daunger quite despise,
Toward those parts came flying careleslie,
Where hidden was his hatefull enemie.

Who, seeing him, with secrete joy therefore
Did tickle inwardly in everie vaine,
And his false hart, fraught with all treasons store,
Was fil'd with hope his purpose to obtaine:
Himselfe he close upgathered more and more
Into his den, that his deceiptfull traine
By his there being might not be bewraid,
Ne anie noyse, ne anie motion made.

Like as a wily foxe, that, having spide
Where on a sunnie banke the lambes doo play,
Full closely creeping by the hinder side,
Lyes in ambushment of his hoped pray,
Ne stirreth limbe, till, seeing readie tide,
He rusheth forth, and snatcheth quite away
One of the litle younglings unawares:
So to his worke Aragnoll him prepares.

Who now shall give unto my heavie eyes
A well of teares, that all may overflow?
Or where shall I finde lamentable cryes,
And mournfull tunes enough my griefe to show?
Helpe, O thou Tragick Muse, me to devise
Notes sad enough, t' expresse this bitter throw:
For loe! the drerie stownd is now arrived,
That of all happines hath us deprived.

The luckles Clarion, whether cruell Fate
Or wicked Fortune faultles him misled,
Or some ungracious blast out of the gate
Of Aeoles raine perforce him drove on hed,
Was (O sad hap and howre unfortunate!)
With violent swift flight forth caried
Into the cursed cobweb, which his foe

Had framed for his finall overthroe.

There the fond flie, entangled, strugled long,
Himselfe to free thereout; but all in vaine.
For, striving more, the more in laces strong
Himselfe he tide, and wrapt his winges twaine
In lymie snares the subtill loupes among;
That in the ende he breathelesse did remaine,
And all his yougthly forces idly spent
Him to the mercie of th' avenger lent.

Which when the greisly tyrant did espie,
Like a grimme lyon rushing with fierce might
Out of his den, he seized greedelie
On the resistles pray, and with fell spight,
Under the left wing stroke his weapon slie
Into his heart, that his deepe groning spright
In bloodie streames foorth fled into the aire,
His bodie left the spectacle of care.

FINIS.

VISIONS OF THE WORLDS VANITIE

This series of original 'visions' is manifestly of kin to those translated from Petrarch and Du Bellay and, more distantly, to 'Ruins of Rome.' It is unquestionably of later composition, but how much later has been disputed. Some critics, observing that, whereas the sonnets of the three earlier series are in the common Elizabethan form, the sonnets of this are in the special form that Spenser devised for himself, have argued that the interval of time must be considerable. In the first place, however, we have no proof that Spenser may not have devised his own sonnet-form early (we meet it in the dedication to 'Virgil's Gnat,' of Calendar days); in the second place, for the three series that were translations he might naturally choose the looser and therefore easier Elizabethan form, when, for original sonnets, he would adopt his own more complicated scheme. This point set aside, there is nothing in the series to denote a much later period: the style is, indeed, distinctly immature. One may plausibly conclude that 'Visions of the World's Vanity' was suggested by the earlier 'Visions' and executed not long after them.

The noteworthy fact about these various early poems is that they show Spenser, at the outset of his career, driving full on allegory. Partly by accident and partly by choice, he has committed himself to a special form of the art, from which he later progresses to others more comprehensive. This form is the literary counterpart of a mixed type, in which poetry and the graphic arts are combined, the so-called 'emblem.' The essence of both consists in the expression of an idea by means of a complete image or picture. Thus Du Bellay, having composed in his Antiquitez de Rome ('Ruins of Rome') a series of meditations upon the transitoriness of human grandeur, went on, in his supplementary Songe ('Visions of Bellay'), to express those same ideas in a series of poetic pictures. These, when borrowed by Van der Noot for the Théâtre of 1568, were made into emblems proper by the addition of engravings that rendered them to the eye. Such emblem books, of engravings and poetry combined, were enormously popular through most of the sixteenth century. They affected the imagination of that period incalculably. Book followed book, edition edition. Mythology, fable, natural history, history were ransacked for themes and illustrations, which were repeated in a dozen forms. Poetry, which, as the 'Visions of Petrarch' show, had long since practised a variety of this art, was stimulated to it afresh. Spenser, in his turn, wrote 'Visions of the World's Vanity,' among which the sonnets on the Scarabee and the Remora, adapted from the first great emblem-writer Alciati, sufficiently declare his indebtedness. The influence may be thought to extend even to the allegory of the Faery Queen; for the figures in the procession at the House of Pride and in the Masque of Cupid, with others of their kind, are in a way but figures from the emblem books glorified by a larger art. At this point, however, the emblem as a special type merges in the more common forms of allegory

I

One day, whiles that my daylie cares did sleepe,
My spirit, shaking off her earthly prison,
Began to enter into meditation deepe
Of things exceeding reach of common reason;
Such as this age, in which all good is geason,
And all that humble is and meane debaced,
Hath brought forth in her last declining season,
Griefe of good mindes, to see goodnesse disgraced.
On which when as my thought was throghly placed,
Unto my eyes strange showes presented were,
Picturing that which I in minde embraced,
That yet those sights empassion me full nere.
Such as they were (faire Ladie) take in worth,
That when time serves, may bring things better forth.

II

In summers day, when Phœbus fairly shone,
I saw a bull as white as driven snowe,
With gilden hornes embowed like the moone,
In a fresh flowring meadow lying lowe:
Up to his eares the verdant grasse did growe,
And the gay floures did offer to be eaten;
But he with fatnes so did overflowe,
That he all wallowed in the weedes downe beaten,
Ne car'd with them his daintie lips to sweeten:
Till that a brize, a scorned little creature,
Through his faire hide his angrie sting did threaten,
And vext so sore, that all his goodly feature
And all his plenteous pasture nought him pleased:
So by the small the great is oft diseased.

III

Beside the fruitfull shore of muddie Nile,
Upon a sunnie banke outstretched lay,
In monstrous length, a mightie crocodile,
That, cram'd with guiltles blood and greedie pray
Of wretched people travailing that way,
Thought all things lesse than his disdainfull pride.
I saw a little bird, cal'd Tedula,
The least of thousands which on earth abide,

That forst this hideous beast to open wide
The greisly gates of his devouring hell,
And let him feede, as Nature doth provide,
Upon his jawes, that with blacke venime swell.
Why then should greatest things the least disdaine,
Sith that so small so mightie can constraine?

IV
The kingly bird, that beares Joves thunderclap,
One day did scorne the simple scarabee,
Proud of his highest service and good hap,
That made all other foules his thralls to bee:
The silly flie, that no redresse did see,
Spide where the eagle built his towring nest,
And kingling fire within the hollow tree,
Burnt up his yong ones, and himselfe distrest;
Ne suffred him in anie place to rest,
But drove in Joves owne lap his egs to lay;
Where gathering also filth him to infest,
Forst with the filth his egs to fling away:
For which when as the foule was wroth, said Jove,
'Lo! how the least the greatest may reprove.'

V
Toward the sea turning my troubled eye,
I saw the fish (if fish I may it cleepe)
That makes the sea before his face to flye,
And with his flaggie finnes doth seeme to sweepe
The fomie waves out of the dreadfull deep,
The huge Leviathan, Dame Natures wonder,
Making his sport, that manie makes to weep:
A sword-fish small him from the rest did sunder,
That, in his throat him pricking softly under,
His wide abysse him forced forth to spewe,
That all the sea did roare like heavens thunder,
And all the waves were stain'd with filthie hewe.
Hereby I learned have, not to despise
What ever thing seemes small in common eyes.

VI
An hideous dragon, dreadfull to behold,
Whose backe was arm'd against the dint of speare
With shields of brasse, that shone like burnisht golde,
And forkhed sting, that death in it did beare,
Strove with a spider, his unequall peare,
And bad defiance to his enemie.
The subtill vermin, creeping closely neare,
Did in his drinke shed poyson privilie;
Which, through his entrailes spredding diversly,
Made him to swell, that nigh his bowells brust,
And him enforst to yeeld the victorie,

That did so much in his owne greatnesse trust.
O how great vainnesse is it then to scorne
The weake, that hath the strong so oft forlorne!

VII
High on a hill a goodly cedar grewe,
Of wondrous length and streight proportion,
That farre abroad her daintie odours threwe;
Mongst all the daughters of proud Libanon,
Her match in beautie was not anie one.
Shortly within her inmost pith there bred
A litle wicked worme, perceiv'd of none,
That on her sap and vitall moysture fed:
Thenceforth her garland so much honoured
Began to die, (O great ruth for the same!)
And her faire lockes fell from her loftie head,
That shortly balde and bared she became.
I, which this sight beheld, was much dismayed,
To see so goodly thing so soone decayed.

VIII
Soone after this I saw an elephant,
Adorn'd with bells and bosses gorgeouslie,
That on his backe did beare (as batteilant)
A gilden towre, which shone exceedinglie;
That he himselfe through foolish vanitie,
Both for his rich attire and goodly forme,
Was puffed up with passing surquedrie,
And shortly gan all other beasts to scorne:
Till that a little ant, a silly worme,
Into his nosthrils creeping, so him pained,
That, casting downe his towres, he did deforme
Both borrowed pride, and native beautie stained.
Let therefore nought, that great is, therein glorie,
Sith so small thing his happines may varie.

IX
Looking far foorth into the ocean wide,
A goodly ship with banners bravely dight,
And flag in her top-gallant, I espide,
Through the maine sea making her merry flight:
Faire blew the winde into her bosome right,
And th' heavens looked lovely all the while,
That she did seeme to daunce, as in delight,
And at her owne felicitie did smile.
All sodainely there clove unto her keele
A little fish, that men call Remora,
Which stopt her course, and held her by the heele,
That winde nor tide could move her thence away.
Straunge thing me seemeth, that so small a thing
Should able be so great an one to wring.

X

A mighty lyon, lord of all the wood,
Having his hunger throughly satisfide
With pray of beasts and spoyle of living blood,
Safe in his dreadles den him thought to hide:
His sternesse was his prayse, his strength his pride,
And all his glory in his cruell clawes.
I saw a wasp, that fiercely him defide,
And bad him battaile even to his jawes;
Sore he him stong, that it the blood forth drawes,
And his proude heart is fild with fretting ire:
In vaine he threats his teeth, his tayle, his pawes,
And from his bloodie eyes doth sparkle fire;
That dead himselfe he wisheth for despight.
So weakest may anoy the most of might.

XI

What time the Romaine Empire bore the raine
Of all the world, and florisht most in might,
The nations gan their soveraigntie disdaine,
And cast to quitt them from their bondage quight:
So, when all shrouded were in silent night,
The Galles were, by corrupting of a mayde,
Possest nigh of the Capitol through slight,
Had not a goose the treachery bewrayde.
If then a goose great Rome from ruine stayde,
And Jove himselfe, the patron of the place,
Preservd from being to his foes betrayde,
Why do vaine men mean things so much deface,
And in their might repose their most assurance,
Sith nought on earth can chalenge long endurance?

XII

When these sad sights were overpast and gone,
My spright was greatly moved in her rest,
With inward ruth and deare affection,
To see so great things by so small distrest:
Thenceforth I gan in my engrieved brest
To scorne all difference of great and small,
Sith that the greatest often are opprest,
And unawares doe into daunger fall.
And ye, that read these ruines tragicall,
Learne by their losse to love the low degree,
And if that Fortune chaunce you up to call
To honours seat, forget not what you be:
For he that of himselfe is most secure
Shall finde his state most fickle and unsure.

FINIS.

'The Visions of Bellay' and 'The Visions of Petrarch,' which belong together, are presumably the earliest poems of the volume. They are but a remodelling of Spenser's first known literary work, the translation done in for Van der Noot's Theatre: it is more than likely, therefore, that they were executed while that work was still of interest to him, during his early days at Cambridge. The object of the youthful poet in these rifacimenti was apparently not to better his translation, but, for merely artistic effect, to turn the irregular stanzas of the Petrarch group and the blank verse poems of the Bellay group into formal sonnets. He does not seem to have consulted his foreign originals afresh, except that he here renders for the first time four sonnets out of Du Bellay which Van der Noot, in transferring the Frenchman's series to his book, had dropped. The version of will be found in the Appendix.

I

It was the time when rest, soft sliding downe
From heavens hight into mens heavy eyes,
In the forgetfulnes of sleepe doth drowne
The carefull thoughts of mortall miseries.
Then did a ghost before mine eyes appeare,
On that great rivers banck, that runnes by Rome,
Which, calling me by name, bad me to reare
My lookes to heaven, whence all good gifts do come,
And crying lowd, 'Loe now, beholde,' quoth hee,
'What under this great temple placed is:
Lo, all is nought but flying vanitee!'
So I, that know this worlds inconstancies,
Sith onely God surmounts all times decay,
In God alone my confidence do stay.

II

On high hills top I saw a stately frame,
An hundred cubits high by just assize,
With hundreth pillours fronting faire the same,
All wrought with diamond after Dorick wize:
Nor brick, nor marble was the wall in view,
But shining christall, which from top to base
Out of her womb a thousand rayons threw
On hundred steps of Afrike golds enchase:
Golde was the parget, and the seeling bright
Did shine all scaly with great plates of golde;
The floore of jasp and emeraude was dight.
O worlds vainesse! Whiles thus I did behold,
An earthquake shooke the hill from lowest seat,
And overthrew this frame with ruine great.

III

Then did a sharped spyre of diamond bright,

Ten feete each way in square, appeare to mee,
Justly proportion'd up unto his hight,
So far as archer might his level see:
The top thereof a pot did seeme to beare,
Made of the mettall which we most do honour,
And in this golden vessell couched weare
The ashes of a mightie emperour:
Upon foure corners of the base were pight,
To beare the frame, foure great lyons of gold;
A worthy tombe for such a worthy wight.
Alas! this world doth nought but grievance hold.
I saw a tempest from the heavenn descend,
Which this brave monument with flash did rend.

IV

I saw raysde up on yvorie pillours tall,
Whose bases were of richest mettalls warke,
The chapters alabaster, the fryses christall,
The double front of a triumphall arke:
On each side purtraid was a Victorie,
Clad like a nimph, that wings of silver weares,
And in triumphant chayre was set on hie
The auncient glory of the Romaine peares.
No worke it seem'd of earthly craftsmans wit,
But rather wrought by his owne industry,
That thunder-dartes for Jove his syre doth fit.
Let me no more see faire thing under sky,
Sith that mine eyes have seene so faire a sight
With sodain fall to dust consumed quight.

V

Then was the faire Dodonian tree far seene
Upon seaven hills to spread his gladsome gleame,
And conquerours bedecked with his greene,
Along the bancks of the Ausonian streame:
There many an auncient trophee was addrest,
And many a spoyle, and many a goodly show,
Which that brave races greatnes did attest,
That whilome from the Troyan blood did flow.
Ravisht I was so rare a thing to vew;
When lo! a barbarous troupe of clownish fone
The honour of these noble boughs down threw:
Under the wedge I heard the tronck to grone;
And since, I saw the roote in great disdaine
A twinne of forked trees send forth againe.

VI

I saw a wolfe under a rockie cave
Noursing two whelpes; I saw her litle ones
In wanton dalliance the teate to crave,
While she her neck wreath'd from them for the nones.

I saw her raunge abroad to seeke her food,
And roming through the field with greedie rage
T' embrew her teeth and clawes with lukewarm blood
Of the small heards, her thirst for to asswage.
I saw a thousand huntsmen, which descended
Downe from the mountaines bordring Lombardie,
That with an hundred speares her flank wide rended:
I saw her on the plaine outstretched lie,
Throwing out thousand throbs in her owne soyle:
Soone on a tree uphang'd I saw her spoyle.

VII
I saw the bird that can the sun endure
With feeble wings assay to mount on hight;
By more and more she gan her wings t' assure,
Following th' ensample of her mothers sight:
I saw her rise, and with a larger flight
To pierce the cloudes, and with wide pinneons
To measure the most haughtie mountaines hight,
Untill she raught the gods owne mansions:
There was she lost; when suddaine I behelde,
Where, tumbling through the ayre in firie fold,
All flaming downe she on the plaine was felde,
And soone her bodie turn'd to ashes colde.
I saw the foule that doth the light dispise
Out of her dust like to a worme arise.

VIII
I saw a river swift, whose fomy billowes
Did wash the ground work of an old great wall;
I saw it cover'd all with griesly shadowes,
That with black horror did the ayre appall:
Thereout a strange beast with seven heads arose,
That townes and castles under her brest did coure,
And seem'd both milder beasts and fiercer foes
Alike with equall ravine to devoure.
Much was I mazde, to see this monsters kinde
In hundred formes to change his fearefull hew;
When as at length I saw the wrathfull winde,
Which blows cold storms, burst out of Scithian mew,
That sperst these cloudes, and in so short as thought,
This dreadfull shape was vanished to nought.

IX
Then all astoined with this mighty ghoast,
An hideous bodie, big and strong, I sawe,
With side long beard, and locks down hanging loast,
Sterne face, and front full of Saturnlike awe;
Who, leaning on the belly of a pot,
Pourd foorth a water, whose out gushing flood
Ran bathing all the creakie shore aflot,

Whereon the Troyan prince spilt Turnus blood;
And at his feete a bitch wolfe suck did yeeld
To two young babes: his left the palme tree stout,
His right hand did the peacefull olive wield,
And head with lawrell garnisht was about.
Sudden both palme and olive fell away,
And faire greene lawrell branch did quite decay.

X

Hard by a rivers side a virgin faire,
Folding her armes to heaven with thousand throbs,
And outraging her cheekes and golden haire,
To falling rivers sound thus tun'd her sobs.
'Where is,' quoth she, 'this whilom honoured face?
Where the great glorie and the auncient praise,
In which all worlds felicitie had place,
When gods and men my honour up did raise?
Suffisd' it not that civill warres me made
The whole worlds spoile, but that this Hydra new,
Of hundred Hercules to be assaide,
With seven heads, budding monstrous crimes anew,
So many Neroes and Caligulaes
Out of these crooked shores must dayly rayse?'

XI

Upon an hill a bright flame I did see,
Waving aloft with triple point to skie,
Which, like incense of precious cedar tree,
With balmie odours fil'd th' ayre farre and nie.
A bird all white, well feathered on each wing,
Hereout up to the throne of gods did flie,
And all the way most pleasant notes did sing,
Whilst in the smoake she unto heaven did stie.
Of this faire fire the scattered rayes forth threw
On everie side a thousand shining beames:
When sudden dropping of a silver dew
(O grievous chance!) gan quench those precious flames;
That it, which earst so pleasant sent did yeld,
Of nothing now but noyous sulphure smeld.

XII

I saw a spring out of a rocke forth rayle,
As cleare as christall gainst the sunnie beames,
The bottome yeallow, like the golden grayle
That bright Pactolus washeth with his streames:
It seem'd that Art and Nature had assembled
All pleasure there, for which mans hart could long;
And there a noyse alluring sleepe soft trembled,
Of manie accords, more sweete than mermaids song:
The seates and benches shone as yvorie,
And hundred nymphes sate side by side about:

When from nigh hills, with hideous outcrie,
A troupe of satyres in the place did rout,
Which with their villeine feete the streame did ray,
Threw down the seats, and drove the nymphs away.

XIII
Much richer then that vessell seem'd to bee,
Which did to that sad Florentine appeare,
Casting mine eyes farre off, I chaunst to see
Upon the Latine coast herselfe to reare.
But suddenly arose a tempest great,
Bearing close envie to these riches rare,
Which gan assaile this ship with dreadfull threat,
This ship, to which none other might compare.
And finally the storme impetuous
Sunke up these riches, second unto none,
Within the gulfe of greedie Nereus.
I saw both ship and mariners each one,
And all that treasure, drowned in the maine:
But I the ship saw after raisd' againe.

XIV
Long having deeply gron'd these visions sad,
I saw a citie like unto that same,
Which saw the messenger of tidings glad,
But that on sand was built the goodly frame:
It seem'd her top the firmament did rayse,
And no lesse rich than faire, right worthie sure
(If ought here worthie) of immortall dayes,
Or if ought under heaven might firme endure.
Much wondred I to see so faire a wall:
When from the Northerne coast a storme arose,
Which, breathing furie from his inward gall
On all which did against his course oppose,
Into a clowde of dust sperst in the aire
The weake foundations of this citie faire.

XV
At length, even at the time when Morpheus
Most trulie doth unto our eyes appeare,
Wearie to see the heavens still wavering thus,
I saw Typhæus sister comming neare;
Whose head, full bravely with a morion hidd,
Did seeme to match the gods in majestie.
She, by a rivers bancke that swift downe slidd,
Over all the world did raise a trophee hie;
An hundred vanquisht kings under her lay,
With armes bound at their backs in shamefull wize.
Whilst I thus mazed was with great affray,
I saw the heavens in warre against her rize:
Then downe she stricken fell with clap of thonder,

That with great noyse I wakte in sudden wonder.

FINIS.

THE VISIONS OF PETRARCH

FORMERLY TRANSLATED

I
Being one day at my window all alone,
So manie strange things happened me to see,
As much it grieveth me to thinke thereon.
At my right hand a hynde appear'd to mee,
So faire as mote the greatest god delite;
Two eager dogs did her pursue in chace,
Of which the one was blacke, the other white:
With deadly force so in their cruell race
They pincht the haunches of that gentle beast,
That at the last, and in short time, I spide,
Under a rocke, where she, alas! opprest,
Fell to the ground, and there untimely dide.
Cruell death vanquishing so noble beautie
Oft makes me wayle so hard a destenie.

II
After, at sea a tall ship did appeare,
Made all of heben and white yvorie;
The sailes of golde, of silke the tackle were:
Milde was the winde, calme seem'd the sea to bee,
The skie eachwhere did show full bright and faire:
With rich treasures this gay ship fraighted was:
But sudden storme did so turmoyle the aire,
And tumbled up the sea, that she (alas!)
Strake on a rock, that under water lay,
And perished past all recoverie.
O how great ruth, and sorrowfull assay,
Doth vex my spirite with perplexitie,
Thus in a moment to see lost and drown'd
So great riches as like cannot be found!

III
Then heavenly branches did I see arise
Out of the fresh and lustie lawrell tree,
Amidst the yong greene wood: of Paradise
Some noble plant I thought my selfe to see.
Such store of birds therein yshrowded were,
Chaunting in shade their sundrie melodie,
That with their sweetnes I was ravish't nere.
While on this lawrell fixed was mine eie,

The skie gan everie where to overcast,
And darkned was the welkin all about:
When sudden flash of heavens fire out brast,
And rent this royall tree quite by the roote;
Which makes me much and ever to complaine;
For no such shadow shalbe had againe.

IV

Within this wood, out of a rocke did rise
A spring of water, mildly rumbling downe,
Whereto approched not in anie wise
The homely shepheard, nor the ruder clowne;
But manie Muses, and the nymphes withall,
That sweetly in accord did tune their voyce
To the soft sounding of the waters fall,
That my glad hart thereat did much rejoyce.
But while herein I tooke my chiefe delight,
I saw (alas!) the gaping earth devoure
The spring, the place, and all cleane out of sight:
Which yet aggreeves my hart even to this houre,
And wounds my soule with rufull memorie,
To see such pleasures gon so suddenly.

V

I saw a phœnix in the wood alone,
With purple wings, and crest of golden hewe;
Strange bird he was, whereby I thought anone,
That of some heavenly wight I had the vewe;
Until he came unto the broken tree,
And to the spring, that late devoured was.
What say I more? Each thing at last we see
Doth passe away: the phœnix there, alas!
Spying the tree destroid, the water dride,
Himselfe smote with his beake, as in disdaine,
And so foorthwith in great despight he dide:
That yet my heart burnes in exceeding paine,
For ruth and pitie of so haples plight.
O, let mine eyes no more see such a sight!

VI

At last, so faire a ladie did I spie,
That thinking yet on her I burne and quake:
On hearbs and flowres she walked pensively,
Milde, but yet love she proudly did forsake:
White seem'd her robes, yet woven so they were
As snow and golde together had been wrought:
Above the wast a darke clowde shrouded her,
A stinging serpent by the heele her caught;
Wherewith she languisht as the gathered floure,
And well assur'd she mounted up to joy.
Alas! on earth so nothing doth endure,

But bitter griefe and sorrowfull annoy:
Which make this life wretched and miserable,
Tossed with stormes of fortune variable.

VII
When I behold this tickle trustles state
Of vaine worlds glorie, flitting too and fro,
And mortall men tossed by troublous fate
In restles seas of wretchednes and woe,
I wish I might this wearie life forgoe,
And shortly turne unto my happie rest,
Where my free spirite might not anie moe
Be vext with sights, that doo her peace molest.
And ye, faire Ladie, in whose bounteous brest
All heavenly grace and vertue shrined is,
When ye these rythmes doo read, and vew the rest,
Loath this base world, and thinke of heavens blis:
And though ye be the fairest of Gods creatures,
Yet thinke, that death shall spoyle your goodly features.

Edmund Spenser – A Short Biography

One of the greatest of English poets, Edmund Spenser was born in East Smithfield, London, in 1552, though an exact date is not recorded.

As a boy, he was educated in London at the Merchant Taylors' School and later at Pembroke College, Cambridge.

As a young man, in 1578, the young Edmund was, for a short time, secretary to John Young, the Bishop of Rochester.

In 1579, he published The Shepheardes Calender, his first major work. The poem follows Colin Clout, a folk character originated by John Skelton, and depicts his life as a shepherd through the twelve months of the year.

It is also around this time that Edmund was married for the first time to Machabyas Childe. The union produced two children; Sylvanus and Katherine.

Edmund journeyed to Ireland in July 1580, in the service of the newly appointed Lord Deputy, Arthur Grey, 14th Baron Grey de Wilton. His time included the terrible massacre at the Siege of Smerwick, though this event seems to have settled his views somewhat on Ireland and the Irish. (The Siege of Smerwick took place at Ard na Caithne in 1580, during the Second Desmond Rebellion. A 400–500 strong force of Papal soldiers captured the town but were later forced to retreat to nearby Dún an Óir, where they were besieged by the English Army and eventually surrendered. On the orders of the English Commander most were then massacred).

When Lord Grey was recalled to England, Edmund stayed, having being appointed to several other official posts and lands in the Munster Plantation. Between 1587 and 1589, Spenser acquired his main estate at Kilcolman, near Doneraile in North Cork.

He later bought a second holding to the south, at Rennie, on a rock overlooking the river Blackwater but still in North Cork. Its ruins are still visible today. A short distance away grew a tree, locally known as "Spenser's Oak". Local legend has it that he penned some of The Faerie Queene under this very tree.

This epic poem, The Faerie Queene, is acknowledged as Edmund's masterpiece. The first three books were published in 1590, and a second set of three books were published in 1596. The original idea was for the poem to consist of twelve books. So although the version we publish here is all that he actually wrote it is still one of the longest, and most magnificent, poems in English literature.

The Faerie Queene is a work on several levels of allegory, including as praise of Queen Elizabeth I. The poem follows several knights in an examination of several virtues. In Spenser's "A Letter of the Authors," he states that the entire epic poem is "cloudily enwrapped in allegorical devises," and that the aim behind The Faerie Queene was to "fashion a gentleman or noble person in virtuous and gentle discipline."

On its publication Spenser travelled to London to publish and promote the work. In this endeavour he was successful enough to obtain a life pension of £50 a year from the Queen who did not give these out lightly.

Spenser used a verse form, now called the Spenserian stanza, in The Faerie Queene as well as several others poems. The stanza's main meter is iambic pentameter with a final line in iambic hexameter (having six stresses, known as an Alexandrine). He was also to use his own rhyme scheme for the sonnet. In a Spenserian sonnet, the last line of every stanza is linked with the first line of the next one.

Spenser was well read in classical literature and strove to emulate such Roman poets as Virgil and Ovid, whom he had studied during his schooling.

Indeed the reality is that Spenser, through his great talents, was able to move Poetry in a different direction. It led to him being called a Poet's Poet and brought rich admiration from Milton, Raleigh, Blake, Wordsworth, Keats, Byron, and Lord Tennyson, among others. John Milton in his Areopagitica called Spenser "our sage and serious poet . . . whom I dare be known to think a better teacher than Scotus or Aquinas".

He had hoped this praise and pension might lead to a position at Court but his next work antagonised the queen's principal secretary, Lord Burghley, through the inclusion of the satirical Mother Hubberd's Tale.

Spenser returned to Ireland and in 1591, Complaints, a collection of poems that voices complaints in mournful or mocking tones was published.

By 1594, Spenser's first wife, Machabyas, had died. Very soon he married Elizabeth Boyle, and to which he dedicated the sonnet sequence Amoretti. The marriage itself was celebrated in Epithalamion and the fruit of this relationship was a son, Peregrine.

In 1595, Spenser now published Amoretti and Epithalamion. The volume contains eighty-nine sonnets.

In the following year Spenser released Prothalamion, a wedding song written for the daughters of a duke, allegedly in hopes to gain favour in the court. More importantly he also wrote a prose pamphlet titled A View of the Present State of Ireland (A Veue of the Present State of Irelande). It was circulated in manuscript form due to its highly inflammatory content. Its main argument was that Ireland would never be totally 'pacified' by the English until its indigenous language and customs had been destroyed, if necessary by violence.

Spenser was a strong proponent of, and wished devoutly, that the Irish language should be eradicated, writing that if children learn Irish before English, "Soe that the speach being Irish, the hart must needes be Irishe; for out of the aboundance of the hart, the tonge speaketh".

He further discussed in the pamphlet future draconian plans to subjugate Ireland, after the most recent rising, led by Hugh O'Neill, having again shown the failure of previous efforts. The work is also a partial defence of Lord Arthur Grey de Wilton, with whom Spenser previously served and who deeply influenced Spenser's views on Ireland.

The goal of this piece was to show that Ireland was in great need of reform. Spenser believed that "Ireland is a diseased portion of the State, it must first be cured and reformed, before it could be in a position to appreciate the good sound laws and blessings of the nation". Spenser categorises the "evils" of the Irish people into three distinct categories: laws, customs, and religion. These three elements work together in creating the disruptive and degraded people. One example given in the work is the native law system called "Brehon Law" which trumps the established law given by the English monarchy. This system has its own court and way of dealing with troubles. It has been passed down through the generations and Spenser views this system as a native and backward custom which must be destroyed. (As an example the Brehon Law methods of dealing with murder by imposing an éraic, or fine, on the murderer's whole family particularly horrified the English, in whose Protestant view a murderer should die for his act.)

He pressed for a scorched earth policy in Ireland, noting that the destruction of crops and animals had been successful in crushing the Second Desmond Rebellion of which he was a part.

However in 1598, during the Nine Years War, Spenser was, ironically, driven from his home by the native Irish forces of Aodh Ó Néill. His castle at Kilcolman was burned.

In 1599, Spenser travelled to London, where he died on January 13th at the age of forty-six. According to Ben Jonson, in another and tragic irony it was "for want of bread".

Edmund Spenser's coffin was carried to his grave in Westminster Abbey by other poets, who threw many pens and pieces of poetry into his grave followed with many tears.

His second wife, Elizabeth, survived him and went on to remarry twice.

Spenser was called a Poets' Poet and was admired by John Milton, William Blake, William Wordsworth, John Keats, Lord Byron, and Alfred Lord Tennyson, among others. Walter Raleigh wrote a dedicatory poem to The Faerie Queene in 1590, in which he claims to admire and value Spenser's work more so than any other in the English language. John Milton in his Areopagitica called Spenser "our sage and serious poet . . . whom I dare be known to think a better teacher than Scotus or Aquinas".

It is praise indeed and clearly shows why Edmund Spenser is indeed part of the Pantheon of our greatest Poets.

1569 - Jan van der Noodt's A theatre for Worldlings, including poems translated into English by Spenser from French sources.

1579 - The Shepheardes Calender, published under the pseudonym "Immerito".

1580 - Three proper, and wittie, familar letters

1590 - The Faerie Queene, Books I–III

1591 - Complaints, Containing sundrie small Poemes of the Worlds Vanitie

1592 - Axiochus, a translation of a pseudo-Platonic dialogue from the original Ancient Greek; attributed to "Edw: Spenser" but the attribution is uncertain

1592 - Daphnaïda. An Elegy upon the death of the noble and vertuous Douglas Howard, Daughter and heire of Henry Lord Howard, Viscount Byndon, and wife of Arthure Gorges Esquier

1595 - Amoretti and Epithalamion

1595 - Astrophel. A Pastorall Elegie vpon the death of the most Noble and valorous Knight, Sir Philip Sidney.

1595 - Colin Clouts Come home againe

1596 - Four Hymns (poem) | Fowre Hymnes dedicated from the court at Greenwich.

1596 - Prothalamion

1596 - The Faerie Queene, Books IV-VI

1598 - A Veue of the Present State of Irelande (Manuscript)

1599 - Babel, Empress of the East – a dedicatory poem prefaced to Lewes Lewkenor's The Commonwealth of Venice.

1609 - Two Cantos of Mutabilitie published together with a reprint of The Fairie Queene.

1611 - First folio edition of Spenser's collected works

1633 - A Veue of the Present State of Irelande, a prose treatise on the reformation of Ireland.